GRAMMAR
Form and Function

2B

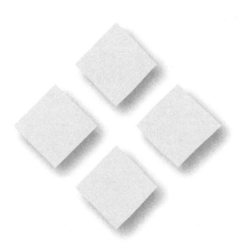

Milada Broukal

**McGraw-Hill
ESL/ELT**

Published by McGraw-Hill ESL/ELT, a business unit of The McGraw-Hill Companies, Inc., 1221 Avenue of the Americas, New York, NY 10020. Copyright © 2004 by The McGraw-Hill Companies, Inc. All rights reserved. No part of this publication may be reproduced or distributed in any form or by any means, or stored in a database or retrieval system, without the prior written consent of The McGraw-Hill Companies, Inc., including, but not limited to, in any network or other electronic storage or transmission, or broadcast for distance learning.

ISBN: 0-07-301378-1

2 3 4 5 6 7 8 9 QPD 9 8 7 6 5 4

Editorial director: Tina B. Carver
Senior managing editor: Erik Gundersen
Developmental editors: Arley Gray, Annie Sullivan
Editorial assistants: David Averbach, Kasey Williamson
Production manager: Juanita Thompson
Cover design: AcentoVisual
Interior design: AcentoVisual
Art: Eldon Doty

Photo credits:
All photos are courtesy of Getty Images Royalty-Free Collection with the exception of the following:
Page 160 © Bettmann/CORBIS; *Page 174* © John Springer Collection/CORBIS; *Page 176* © AFP/CORBIS.

**McGraw-Hill
ESL/ELT**

Contents

UNIT 8 MODAL AUXILIARIES AND RELATED FORMS

UNIT 9 GERUNDS AND INFINITIVES

UNIT 13 ADJECTIVE AND ADVERB CLAUSES

UNIT 14 REPORTED SPEECH AND CONDITIONAL CLAUSES

APPENDICES

Acknowledgements

The publisher and author would like to thank the following individuals who reviewed *Grammar Form and Function* during the development of the series and whose comments and suggestions were invaluable in creating this project.

❖ Tony Albert, *Jewish Vocational Services, San Francisco, CA*

❖ Leslie A. Biaggi, *Miami–Dade Community College, Miami, FL*

❖ Gerry Boyd, *Northern Virginia Community College, VA*

❖ Marcia M. Captan, *Miami–Dade Community College, Miami, FL*

❖ Yongjae Paul Choe, *Dongguk University, Seoul, Korea*

❖ Sally Gearhart, *Santa Rosa Junior College, Santa Rosa, CA*

❖ Mary Gross, *Miramar College, San Diego, CA*

❖ Martin Guerin, *Miami–Dade Community College, Miami, FL*

❖ Patty Heiser, *University of Washington, Seattle, WA*

❖ Susan Kasten, *University of North Texas, Denton, TX*

❖ Sarah Kegley, *Georgia State University, Atlanta, GA*

❖ Kelly Kennedy-Isern, *Miami–Dade Community College, Miami, FL*

❖ Grace Low, *Germantown, TN*

❖ Irene Maksymjuk, *Boston University, Boston, MA*

❖ Christina Michaud, *Bunker Hill Community College, Boston, MA*

❖ Cristi Mitchell, *Miami–Dade Community College-Kendall Campus, Miami, FL*

❖ Carol Piñeiro, *Boston University, Boston, MA*

❖ Michelle Remaud, *Roxbury Community College, Boston, MA*

❖ Diana Renn, *Wentworth Institute of Technology, Boston, MA*

❖ Alice Savage, *North Harris College, Houston, TX*

❖ Karen Stanley, *Central Piedmont Community College, Charlotte, NC*

❖ Roberta Steinberg, *Mt. Ida College, Newton, MA*

The author would like to thank everyone at McGraw-Hill who participated in this project's development, especially Arley Gray, Erik Gundersen, Annie Sullivan, Jennifer Monaghan, David Averbach, Kasey Williamson, and Tina Carver.

Welcome to Grammar Form and Function!

In **Grammar Form and Function 2**, high-interest photos bring intermediate grammar to life, providing visual contexts for learning and retaining new structures and vocabulary.

Welcome to **Grammar Form and Function 2**. This visual tour will provide you with an overview of the key features of a unit.

❖ *Form* presentations teach grammar structures through complete charts and high-interest, memorable photos that facilitate students' recall of grammar structures.

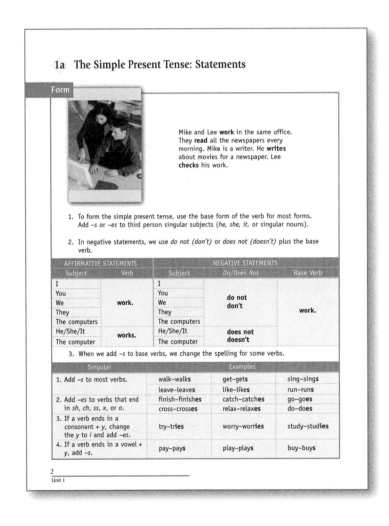

1a The Simple Present Tense: Statements

Form

Mike and Lee **work** in the same office. They **read** all the newspapers every morning. Mike is a writer. He **writes** about movies for a newspaper. Lee **checks** his work.

1. To form the simple present tense, use the base form of the verb for most forms. Add –s or –es to third person singular subjects (*he, she, it,* or singular nouns).

2. In negative statements, we use *do not (don't)* or *does not (doesn't)* plus the base verb.

AFFIRMATIVE STATEMENTS		NEGATIVE STATEMENTS		
Subject	Verb	Subject	Do/Does Not	Base Verb
I		I		
You		You	do not	
We	work.	We	don't	
They		They		work.
The computers		The computers		
He/She/It	works.	He/She/It	does not	
The computer		The computer	doesn't	

3. When we add –s to base verbs, we change the spelling for some verbs.

Singular		Examples	
1. Add –s to most verbs.	walk–walks	get–gets	sing–sings
	leave–leaves	like–likes	run–runs
2. Add –es to verbs that end in *sh, ch, ss, x,* or *o*.	finish–finishes	catch–catches	go–goes
	cross–crosses	relax–relaxes	do–does
3. If a verb ends in a consonant + *y*, change the *y* to *i* and add –es.	try–tries	worry–worries	study–studies
4. If a verb ends in a vowel + *y*, add –s.	pay–pays	play–plays	buy–buys

2
Unit I

4. Two verbs are irregular in the simple present tense, *be* and *have*. Also, *be* forms its negative differently from other verbs.

AFFIRMATIVE STATEMENTS			NEGATIVE STATEMENTS		
	Subject	Verb		Subject	Negative Verb	
Be	I	**am**	late.	I	am not 'm not	late.
	You We They	**are**		You We They	are not 're not aren't	
	He/She/It	**is**		He/She/It	is not 's not isn't	
Have	I You We They	**have**	a problem.	I You We They	**don't have**	a problem.
	He/She/It	**has**		He/She/It	**doesn't have**	

Function

1. We use the simple present tense when we talk about habitual actions and for things that happen all the time or are always true.

    Mike **talks** on the phone a lot.
    He **writes** movie reviews on his computer every day.

2. We use the negative contracted forms *don't* and *doesn't* in speech and informal writing. We use the full forms *do not* and *does not* in formal writing and in speech when we want to emphasize the negative.

    INFORMAL: I'm sorry. I **don't** have time to help you now.
    FORMAL OR EMPHATIC: The president **does not** want this report to be late.

3
The Present Tenses

❖ *Form* presentations also include related grammatical points such as negatives, yes/no questions, wh– questions, and short answers.

❖ *Function* explanations and examples clarify when to use grammar structures.

1 | Practice

Complete the sentences with the correct form of the verb in parentheses. Make the verb negative if the word *not* is in the parentheses.

1. Mike (live) _____lives_____ in New York City.
2. He (have) _____ an apartment near the office.
3. He (not, take) _____ the bus to work.
4. He (walk) _____ to work.
5. Mike (like) _____ his job.
6. He (not, be) _____ an office worker.
7. He (be) _____ a writer.
8. He (write) _____ about movies.
9. He (go) _____ to the movies every day.
10. He (see) _____ new movies.
11. He (have) _____ a small computer.
12. He (take) _____ his computer with him to the movies.
13. He (not, go) _____ home at 5:00 in the afternoon.
14. Mike (work) _____ late.
15. He (sleep) _____ late, too.
16. Lee (correct) _____ his work.
17. They (work) _____ for the same newspaper.
18. Mike and Lee (read) _____ a lot of other newspapers.
19. They (talk) _____ on the phone a lot.
20. They (drink) _____ a lot of coffee, too.
21. Mike and Lee (not, agree) _____ all the time.
22. Lee (not, like) _____ Mike's work all the time.

2 | Your Turn

Think of five activities that a friend does. Tell your partner.

Examples:
My sister teaches art to children.
She drives to work.
She helps the children.
She likes her job.

4
Unit 1

❖ **Extensive practice** through topical exercises guides students from accurate production to fluent use of the grammar.

❖ **Your Turn** activities guide students to practice grammar in personally meaningful conversations.

❖ **Writing assignments build composition skills, such as narrating and describing, through real-life, step-by-step tasks.**

WRITING: Describe a Person

Write a paragraph about your partner.

Step 1. Ask and answer the questions with a partner. Record the answers by checking "Yes" or "No." Write additional information under "Other Information."

	Yes	No	Other Information
1. live/in (city)	_____	_____	_____
2. work	_____	_____	_____
3. like/tennis	_____	_____	_____
4. listen/pop music	_____	_____	_____
5. have/car	_____	_____	_____
6. go/movies on weekends	_____	_____	_____
7. speak/(language)	_____	_____	_____
8. play/the piano	_____	_____	_____
9. go on vacation/in the summer	_____	_____	_____
10. have/brothers and sisters	_____	_____	_____

Step 2. Write sentences about your partner from your notes.

Example:
Kumiko lives in Tokyo.
She doesn't work.
She goes to school.

Step 3. Rewrite the sentences in the form of a paragraph. Write a title (your partner's name). For more writing guidelines, see pages 410–416.

Kumiko Osawa

Kumiko lives in Tokyo She doesn't work because she's a student. She likes...

Step 4. Evaluate your paragraph.

Checklist
_____ Did you indent the first line?
_____ Did you give the paragraph a title?
_____ Did you write the title with a capital letter for each word?

Step 5. Edit your work. Work with a partner or your teacher to edit your sentences. Correct spelling, punctuation, vocabulary, and grammar.

Step 6. Write your final copy.

SELF-TEST

A Choose the best answer, A, B, C, or D, to complete the sentence. Mark your answer by darkening the oval with the same letter.

1. Many animals _____ their young in the spring.

   A. are having   Ⓐ Ⓑ Ⓒ Ⓓ
   B. have
   C. has
   D. is have

2. Every year, the Earth _____ around the Sun one time.

   A. travels   Ⓐ Ⓑ Ⓒ Ⓓ
   B. travel
   C. is traveling
   D. does traveling

3. Snow _____ in the Sahara Desert.

   A. sometimes falls   Ⓐ Ⓑ Ⓒ Ⓓ
   B. sometimes is falling
   C. falls sometimes
   D. is falling sometimes

4. Sharks _____ bones.

   A. do not have   Ⓐ Ⓑ Ⓒ Ⓓ
   B. are not having
   C. have not

6. At the moment, everybody _____ the football game on television.

   A. is seeing   Ⓐ Ⓑ Ⓒ Ⓓ
   B. is watching
   C. is looking at
   D. does watch

7. We _____ vitamins for good health.

   A. are needing   Ⓐ Ⓑ Ⓒ Ⓓ
   B. need have
   C. have need
   D. need

8. Young children _____ the pictures in books.

   A. always look at   Ⓐ Ⓑ Ⓒ Ⓓ
   B. always see
   C. look at always
   D. always watch

9. When _____ breakfast?

   A. you have   Ⓐ Ⓑ Ⓒ Ⓓ
   B. have you
   C. do you have

❖ **Self-Tests** at the end of each unit allow students to evaluate their mastery of the grammar while providing informal practice of standardized test taking.

B Find the underlined word or phrase, A, B, C, or D, that is incorrect. Mark your answer by darkening the oval with the same letter.

1. Italians <u>usually</u> <u>eats</u> pasta <u>every day</u>
           A   B   C
   <u>of the week</u>.
     D

   Ⓐ Ⓑ Ⓒ Ⓓ

2. <u>How many</u> <u>hours</u> does <u>a baby</u> <u>sleeps</u>?
      A   B   C   D

   Ⓐ Ⓑ Ⓒ Ⓓ

3. <u>People</u> catch <u>sometimes</u> <u>colds</u> <u>in the</u> winter.
     A   B   C   D

   Ⓐ Ⓑ Ⓒ Ⓓ

4. <u>Do</u> bears <u>eat</u> only meat, or <u>they do</u> <u>eat</u>
     A   B   C   D
   plants, too?

   Ⓐ Ⓑ Ⓒ Ⓓ

6. In India, the cow <u>gives</u> <u>milk</u> <u>and</u>
                 A   B   C
   <u>is working</u> on the farm.
     D

   Ⓐ Ⓑ Ⓒ Ⓓ

7. Camels <u>do not</u> <u>drink</u> <u>often</u> water for days
            A   B   C
   when they <u>travel</u>.
              D

   Ⓐ Ⓑ Ⓒ Ⓓ

8. When <u>do</u> people <u>use</u> computers, they
         A   B
   <u>often</u> <u>use</u> the Internet to get information.
     C   D

   Ⓐ Ⓑ Ⓒ Ⓓ

9. <u>Men and women</u> in Iceland <u>have</u> long lives
         A   B
   because the air <u>has</u> clean and they <u>have</u>

To the Teacher

Grammar Form and Function is a three-level series designed to ensure students' success in learning grammar. The series features interesting photos to help students accurately recall grammar points, meaningful contexts, and a clear, easy-to-understand format that integrates practice of the rules of essential English grammar (form) with information about when to apply them and what they mean (function).

Features

❖ **Flexible approach to grammar instruction** integrates study of new structures (form) with information on how to use them and what they mean (function).
❖ **High-interest photos** contextualize new grammar and vocabulary.
❖ **Comprehensive grammar coverage** targets all basic structures.
❖ **Extensive practice** ensures accurate production and fluent use of grammar.
❖ **Your Turn activities** guide students to practice grammar in personally meaningful conversations.
❖ **Writing assignments** build composition skills like narrating and describing through step-by-step tasks.
❖ **Self-Tests and Unit Quizzes** offer multiple assessment tools for student and teacher use, in print and Web formats.
❖ **Companion Website activities** develop real-world listening and reading skills.

Components

❖ **Student Book** has 14 units with abundant practice in both form and function of each grammar structure. Each unit also features communicative *Your Turn* activities, a step-by-step *Writing* assignment, and a *Self-Test*.
❖ **Teacher's Manual** provides the following:
   ◆ Teaching tips and techniques
   ◆ Overview of each unit
   ◆ Answer keys for the Student Book and Workbook
   ◆ Expansion activities
   ◆ Culture, usage, and vocabulary notes
   ◆ Answers to frequently asked questions about the grammar structures
   ◆ Unit quizzes in a standardized test format and answer keys for each unit.
❖ **Workbook** features additional exercises for each grammar structure, plus an extra student Self-Test at the end of each unit.
❖ **Website** provides further practice, as well as additional assessments.

Overview of the Series

Pedagogical Approach

What is *form*?

Form is the structure of a grammar point and what it looks like. Practice of the form builds students' accuracy and helps them recognize the grammar point in authentic situations, so they are better prepared to understand what they are reading or what other people are saying.

What is *function*?

Function is when and how we use a grammar point. Practice of the function builds students' fluency and helps them apply the grammar point in their real lives.

Why does **Grammar Form and Function** incorporate both form and function into its approach to teaching grammar?

Mastery of grammar relies on students knowing the rules of English (form) and correctly understanding how to apply them (function). Providing abundant practice in both form and function is key to student success.

How does **Grammar Form and Function** incorporate form and function into its approach to teaching grammar?

For each grammar point, the text follows a consistent format:

❖ **Presentation of Form.** The text presents the complete form, or formal rule, along with several examples for students to clearly see the model. There are also relevant photos to help illustrate the grammar point.

❖ **Presentation of Function.** The text explains the function of the grammar point, or how it is used, along with additional examples for reinforcement.

❖ **Practice.** Diverse exercises practice the form and function together. Practice moves logically from more controlled to less controlled activities.

❖ **Application.** Students apply the grammar point in open-ended communicative activities. **Your Turn** requires students to draw from and speak about personal experiences, and **Writing** provides a variety of writing assignments that rely on communicative group and pair discussions. **Expansion** activities in the Teacher's Manual provide additional creative, fun practice for students.

What is the purpose of the photos in the book?

Most people have a visual memory. When you see a photo aligned with a grammar point, the photo helps you remember and contextualize the grammar. The photo reinforces the learning and retention. If there were no visual image, you'd be more likely to forget the grammar point. For example, let's say you are learning the present progressive. You read the example "She is drinking a glass of water." At the same time, you are shown a photo of a girl drinking a glass of water. Later, you are more likely to recall the form of the present progressive because your mind has made a mental picture that helps you remember.

Practice

How were the grammar points selected?

We did a comprehensive review of courses at this level to ensure that all of the grammar points taught were included.

Does **Grammar Form and Function** have controlled or communicative practice?

It has both. Students practice each grammar point through controlled exercises and then move on to tackle open-ended communicative activities.

Do students have a chance to personalize the grammar?

Yes. There are opportunities to personalize the grammar in **Your Turn** and **Writing**. **Your Turn** requires students to draw from and speak about personal experiences, and **Writing** provides a variety of writing assignments that rely on communicative group and pair discussions.

Does **Grammar Form and Function** help students work toward fluency or accuracy?

Both. The exercises are purposefully designed to increase students' accuracy and enhance their fluency by practicing both form and function. Students' confidence in their accuracy helps boost their fluency.

Why does the text feature writing practice?

Grammar and writing are linked in a natural way. Specific grammar structures lend themselves to specific writing genres. In *Grammar Form and Function*, carefully devised practice helps students keep these structures in mind as they are writing.

In addition to the grammar charts, what other learning aids are in the book?

The book includes 11 pages of appendices that are designed to help the students as they complete the exercises. In addition to grammar resources such as lists of irregular verbs and spelling rules for endings, the appendices also feature useful and interesting information, including grammar terms, rules for capitalization and punctuation, writing basics, and even maps. In effect, the appendices constitute a handbook that students can use not only in grammar class, but in other classes as well.

Are there any additional practice opportunities?

Yes, there are additional exercises in the Workbook and on the Website. There are also **Expansion** activities in the Teacher's Manual that provide more open-ended (and fun!) practice for students.

Assessment

What is the role of student self-assessment in Grammar Form and Function?

Every opportunity for student self-assessment is valuable! *Grammar Form and Function* provides two Self-Tests for each unit – one at the end of each Student Book unit and another at the end of each Workbook unit. The Self-Tests build student confidence, encourage student independence as learners, and increase student competence in following standardized test formats. In addition, the Self-Tests serve as important tools for the teacher in measuring student mastery of grammar structures.

Does Grammar Form and Function offer students practice in standardized test formats?

Yes, the two Self-Tests and the Unit Quiz for each unit all utilize standardized test formats. Teachers may use the three tests in the way that best meets student, teacher, and institutional needs. For example, teachers may first assign the Self-Test in the Workbook as an untimed practice test to be taken at home. Then in the classroom, teachers may administer the Self-Test in the Student Book for a more realistic, but still informal, test-taking experience. Finally, teachers may administer the Unit Quiz from the Teacher's Manual as a more standardized timed test.

How long should each Self-Test or Unit Quiz take?

Since there is flexibility in implementing the Self-Tests and Unit Quizzes, there is also flexibility in the timing of the tests. When used for informal test-taking practice at home or in class, they may be administered as untimed tests. When administered as timed tests in class, they should take no more than 20 minutes.

How can I be sure students have mastered the grammar?

Grammar Form and Function provides a variety of tools to evaluate student mastery of the grammar. Traditional evaluation tools include the practice exercises, Self-Tests, and Unit Quizzes. To present a more complete picture of student mastery, the series also includes **Your Turn** activities and **Writing**, which illustrate how well students have internalized the grammar structures and are able to apply them in realistic tasks. Teachers can use these activities to monitor and assess students' ability to incorporate new grammatical structures into their spoken and written discourse.

Unit Format

What is the unit structure of Grammar Form and Function?

Consult the guide to *Grammar Form and Function* on pages VIII-X. This walkthrough provides a visual tour of a Student Book unit.

How many hours of instruction are in Grammar Form and Function 2?

The key to *Grammar Form and Function* is flexibility! The grammar structures in the Student Book may be taught in order, or teachers may rearrange units into an order that best meets their students' needs. To shorten the number of hours of instruction, teachers may choose not to teach all of the grammar structures, or use all of the exercises provided. On the other hand, teachers may add additional hours by assigning exercises in the Workbook or on the Website. In addition, the Teacher's Manual provides teaching suggestions and expansion activities that would add extra hours of instruction.

Ancillary Components

What can I find in the Teacher's Manual?

❖ Teaching tips and techniques
❖ Overview of each unit
❖ Answer keys for the Student Book and Workbook
❖ Expansion activities
❖ Culture, usage, and vocabulary notes
❖ Answers to frequently asked questions about the grammar structures
❖ Unit quizzes in a standardized test format and quiz answer keys.

How do I supplement classroom instruction with the Workbook?

The Workbook exercises can be used to add instructional hours to the course, to provide homework practice, and to reinforce and refresh the skills of students who have mastered the grammar structures. It also provides additional standardized test-taking practice.

What can students find on the Website?

Students and teachers will find a wealth of engaging listening and reading activities on the *Grammar Form and Function* Website. As with the Workbook, the Website exercises can be used to add instructional hours to the course, to provide homework practice, and to reinforce and refresh the skills of students who have mastered the grammar structures.

UNIT 8

MODAL AUXILIARIES AND RELATED FORMS

8a Can, Could, and Be Able To to Express Ability

Fred **could play** football last year, but he **can't play** football now.

1. We use the modal auxiliary *can* + a base verb to express ability in the present or future, and *could* + a base verb to express ability in the past.

2. Like all modals, *can* and *could* take the same form for all persons. There is no *−s* ending in the third person singular.

3. We put *not* after *can, could,* and other modals to form the negative. Many modals can be contracted in their negative form.

Affirmative	Negative Full Form	Negative Contraction
can	cannot	can't
could	could not	couldn't

Note that the full negative form of *can* is written as one word: *cannot*. The full negative form of other modal auxiliaries is written as two words: *could not; should not.*

CAN: ABILITY IN THE PRESENT OR FUTURE				COULD: ABILITY IN THE PAST			
Subject	Can Cannot Can't	Base Verb		Subject	Could Could Not Couldn't	Base Verb	
I You He/She/It We They	**can cannot can't**	**play**	now. later.	I You He/She/It We They	**could could not couldn't**	**play**	then.

4. We put *can, could,* and other modals before the subject to form questions.

QUESTIONS				SHORT ANSWERS	
Can	Subject	Base Verb		Yes,	No,
Can	I	**play**	now? later?	you can.	you can't.
	you			I/we can.	I/we can't.
	he/she/it			he/she/it can.	he/she/it can't.
	we			you can.	you can't.
	they			they can.	they can't.

5. We can use *be able to* to express ability in the present, past, and future.

ABLE TO: ABILITY IN THE PRESENT				
Subject	Form of *Be*	*Able To*	Base Verb	
I	**am**	**able to**	**play**	now.
You	**are**			
He/She/It	**is**			
We	**are**			
They				

ABLE TO: ABILITY IN THE PAST				
Subject	Form of *Be*	*Able To*	Base Verb	
I	**was**	**able to**	**play**	yesterday.
You	**were**			
He/She/It	**was**			
We	**were**			
They				

ABLE TO: ABILITY IN THE FUTURE				
Subject	Form of *Be*	*Able To*	Base Verb	
I	**will be**	**able to**	**play**	tomorrow.
You				
He/She/It				
We				
They				

1. We use *can* + a base verb to express ability in the present or future.

    She **can speak** Japanese.
    He **can play** tennis very well.
    I **can help** you in 15 minutes.

2. We use *could* + a base verb to express ability in the past.

    When I was young, I **could run** five miles.
    I **couldn't drive** five years ago.

3. *Am/is/are able to* and *was/were able to* have the same general meaning as *can* and *could. Can* and *could* are more common in speech.

    I wanted to call you, but I **couldn't remember** your phone number.
    I wanted to call you, but I **wasn't able to remember** your phone number.

4. When we want to suggest that something is frustrating or difficult, we usually use *be able to.*

    I tried very hard, but I **wasn't able to do** all of my math problems.
    After I spoke to my teacher, I **was able to do** them.

5. When we talk about a future ability that we do not have in the present, we use *will be able to.*

    Next year, **I'll be able to drive.**

6. We must use *be able to,* not *can,* with some grammatical structures, such as with another modal and in the present perfect tense.

    CORRECT: You should be able to do this problem.
    INCORRECT: You ~~should can~~ do this problem.

    CORRECT: I have been able to swim since I was six.
    INCORRECT: I ~~can have swum~~ since I was six.

I   Practice

Fred has a broken leg and broken arms. What can he do? What can't he do?
Complete the sentences with *can* or *can't* and one of the verbs from the list.

eat	listen	shake	watch
hold	put on	talk	wear

1. He ___can't wear___ his shoes.
2. He _____ his meals by himself.
3. He _____ a glass of water in his hands.
4. He _____ hands with visitors.
5. He _____ television.
6. He _____ to the doctors and nurses and visitors.
7. He _____ his clothes by himself.
8. He _____ to the radio.

2 | Practice

Complete the sentences with *could* or *couldn't*.

Tarzan was a human who was born in a jungle. He ___could___ survive there
                                                    1
because apes took care of him as their own baby. As Tarzan grew, he _____
                                                                           2
do many things that the apes _____ do. He _____ climb
                                    3   4
trees. He _____ swing from tree to tree. He _____ find nuts
              5   6
and fruit to eat.

One day, some European men in the jungle saw the strange man. They _____
                                                                          7
understand how he lived there. They tried to speak with him, but he _____
                                                                          8
speak. He _____ make only animal noises. The men took Tarzan
              9
back to Europe with them. They taught him many things. After some time, he
_____ speak French. He _____ also walk and eat like other
      10   11
people in Europe.

3 | What Do You Think?

1. What other things could Tarzan do in the jungle?
2. What things could he do after he lived in Europe for a while?

4 | Your Turn

You are going on a trip to the jungle for two weeks. Choose six things you need to take with you to survive. What do you need them for? Use *can*.

Example:
I need a blanket so I can cover myself at night.

5 Practice

Joe likes outdoor activities. Rewrite the sentences using the correct form of *be able to* in place of *can/could* + a verb.

1. It's summer now. Joe and his friends can play baseball outdoors.

It's summer now. Joe and his friends are able to play baseball outdoors.

2. He can go hiking in the mountains.

_____

3. He can play tennis now, and he can also play it in the fall.

_____

4. He can't go ice skating now, but he could go ice skating last winter.

_____

5. Last winter, he couldn't go skiing because he didn't have the money.

_____

6. He and I can go mountain climbing now.

_____

7. We can't go mountain climbing in the winter because it's too dangerous then.

_____

6 Practice

Check the correct completion for the sentences. Sometimes both choices are possible.

1. √ can't   I ... cook very well, so I'm taking a course.
   √ am not able to

2. ___ can   When I finish this course, I ... make Chinese food.
   ___ will be able to

3. ___ can   I ... make stir-fried dishes now.
   ___ am able to

4. ___ couldn't   Before taking this course, I ... make spaghetti sauce.
   ___ wasn't able to

5. ___ could   I ... learn how to make cakes, but it took me a long time.
   ___ was able to

6. ___ can   If I work hard, I might ... make some French dishes soon.
   ___ be able to

7. ___ will be able to   When this course is over, I ... give my family better meals.
   ___ am able to

8. ___ can   Also, I should ... save money.
   ___ be able to

9. ___ can   My instructor says that you spend less money if you ...
   ___ are able to   cook well.

8b *May I, Could I,* and *Can I* to Ask for Permission

Can I have another napkin?

QUESTIONS			ANSWERS	
Modal	Subject	Base Verb	Affirmative	Negative
May			Yes, of course.	
			Certainly.	I'm sorry. It's for
Could	I	use	the phone?	Sure.*	office use only.
Can			No problem.*	
May	I	help	you?	Yes, please.	No, thanks.
Can					

*These expressions are informal English.

1. We use *may I, can I,* and *could I* + a base verb to ask for permission to do something. *May I* is the most polite, or formal, of the three. We often use *may I* when speaking to someone who is older, who is in authority over us, or whom we do not know.

2. *Could I* is more polite or formal than *can I*. *Could I* is a good choice for most situations.

3. *Can I* is often used between people who know each other well.

In these sentences, a customer asks for a form from a bank teller.

FORMAL   **May I take** one of these?   (They do not know each other.)

       Could I take one of these?   (They might or might not know each other.)

INFORMAL   **Can I take** one of these?   (They have been speaking together or they know each other.)

7 Practice

Complete the conversations with *may I, can I,* or *could I*. In some sentences, there is more than one correct answer.

1. Student: ____May I____ hand in my homework tomorrow, please?

   Teacher: No, you may not.

2. Student: _____ have some more time to finish the essay?

   Teacher: No, absolutely not.

3. Student: _____ borrow your grammar book?

   Classmate: Sure.

4. You: _____ use your computer?

   Classmate: No problem.

5. You: _____ have a scholarship application?

   School Clerk: Sure.

6. You: _____ speak with Professor Jones?

   Secretary: She's not here right now. _____ take a message?

Work with a partner. Ask and answer questions with *may I, can I,* **and** *could I.*

Example:
You are at a friend's house. You want to use the phone.
You: Can I use the phone?
Your partner: Yes, sure.

1. You are at a friend's house. You want to use the telephone.
2. You want to sit next to a person you don't know in a fast food restaurant.
3. You are in a restaurant. You ask for the check.
4. You are in a shoe store. You want to try on the black shoes in the window in size 10.
5. You are talking to the teacher. You want to come to class late tomorrow because you have a doctor's appointment.
6. You are at a friend's house. You want a glass of water.
7. The teacher is carrying a lot of books. You want to help her carry the books.
8. You are on the phone with a friend. The doorbell rings. You want to call your friend back later.

8c *Can, Could,* and *Would* to Make Requests

Form

Could you meet me
later for a movie?

QUESTIONS				ANSWERS	
Modal	Subject	Base Verb		Affirmative	Negative
Can				Yes, of course.	Sorry, I can't.
Could	**you**	**wait**	a minute, please?	Certainly.	I'd like to, but I don't have time.
				Sure.*	
Would				Okay.*	
*These expressions are informal English.					

1. We use *would you, could you,* and *can you* + a base verb to ask someone to do something. The meaning of these three modals is the same when we use them to make a request.

2. Although they have the same meaning, *would* and *could* are more formal than *can*. We generally use *could* and *would* when we make requests of strangers, older people, or people in authority. We use *would, could,* and *can* with friends and family members.

   To a stranger: **Could/Would** you **send** the report, please?
   To a friend: **Could/Would/Can** you **come** here for a second?

3. We use *please* to make requests more polite. We use *please* especially with *would* or *could*. *Please* usually comes after the subject or at the end of the sentence. When *please* comes at the end of the sentence, we put a comma before it.

   Would you **please** sign this?
   Could you sign this, **please**?

---

9 | **Practice**

Work with a partner. Make requests with *can you, could you,* and *would you*. More than one answer is possible.

1. You are speaking to your brother.

   You: _____*Can you*_____ hold this for me?

   Brother: Sure.

2. You are speaking to a bank teller.

   You: _____ give me the balance of my checking account,

   please?

   Bank Teller: Certainly. It's $506.25. Is there anything else I can do for you?

3. You are speaking to your boss.

   You: _____ look over this report, please?

   Boss: I can't do it now, but I'll do it as soon as I can.

4. You are speaking to a flight attendant.

   You: _____ bring me some water, please?

   Flight Attendant: Certainly.

5. You are speaking to a doctor.

You: _____ give me the same prescription as last time, please?

Doctor: Of course.

10 Practice

Work with a partner. Make requests and answer them with *can, could,* and *would.* More than one answer is possible.

1. Ask a stranger to ...

a. tell you the way to the exit.

Could you tell me the way to the exit, please?

b. hold the elevator.

_____

2. Ask your roommate to ...

a. answer the door.

_____

b. help you with your homework.

_____

3. Ask your brother to ...

a. turn off the television.

_____

b. carry the groceries for you.

_____

4. Ask a server at a restaurant to ...

a. bring you the menu.

_____

b. tell you about today's special.

_____

5. Ask a travel agent to ...

a. check for the cheapest fare.

_____

b. send you the ticket.

_____

8d *May, Might,* and *Could* to Express Possibility

Form

That's dangerous! He **may fall!**

Subject	Modal (+ *Not*)	Base Verb
I You He/She/It We They	**may** **may not*** **might** **might not*** **could****	**go.**

*In this meaning, we do not contract *may* and *might* with *not*.
**In this meaning, we do not use *could* in the negative.

Function

1. We use *may, might,* or *could* + a base verb to express something that is possible now or in the future. *May, might,* and *could* mean "perhaps."

   She **may fall** and **break** something.
   OR She **might fall** and **break** something.
   OR She **could fall** and **break** something.
   OR **Perhaps** she will fall and break something.

2. Remember, we also use *could* + a base verb to mean past ability, to ask permission, and to make requests. We also use *may* + a base verb to ask for permission.

   I **could run** very fast when I was young.
   Could I **take** one of these?
   Could you **help** me, please?
   May I **take** one of these, please?

3. When expressing possibility, we do not use *may* in Yes/No questions. *Might* can be used in Yes/No questions, but it is very formal.

CORRECT:	Could that answer be correct?
CORRECT (very formal):	Might that answer be correct?
INCORRECT:	~~May~~ that answer be correct?

4. In this meaning, we do not use *could* in the negative.

CORRECT:	Our flight may not be late.
CORRECT:	Our flight might not be late.
INCORRECT:	Our flight ~~could not~~ be late. (This sentence means "It is impossible for our flight to be late.")

11 Practice

Donald worries about everything. Complete the sentences with *may, might,* or *could* and one of the words or phrases from the list. More than one answer is possible.

bite him	divorce him	have an accident
catch a cold	get sunburned	have bacteria in it
crash		

1. He doesn't fly because he thinks the plane _____ *might crash.* _____
2. He doesn't like to go to the beach because he _____
3. He doesn't go to the zoo because he thinks an animal _____
4. He doesn't go out when it's raining because he _____
5. He doesn't drive because he _____
6. He doesn't eat in a restaurant because the food _____
7. He doesn't want to get married because his wife _____

12 Practice

Underline the correct verb in parentheses.

Ann: What's for dinner?

Betty: We (are having / may have) chicken. It's in the oven.
              ‾‾‾‾‾‾‾‾‾
              1

Ann: When will it be ready?

Betty: I'm not sure. It (will / may) be ready in half an hour.
                               2

Ann: What time is John coming?

Betty: I don't know. It depends on the traffic. He (may / will) be late.
                                                                3

Ann: Is Ted coming at 7:00?

Betty: Yes. He called. He's on his way. He (will / may) be here at seven for sure.
                                               4

Ann: Are we having dessert?

Betty: Yes, we (are / might). It's in the refrigerator.
               5

Ann: It's the doorbell. Who can it be?

Betty: I don't know. It (is / may be) Ted.
                         6

13 Practice

Carla and George are waiting for their friend to arrive from the airport. He is late, and
they are getting worried. Read their conversation. Underline the correct form in parentheses. If both forms are possible, underline both of them.

George: (Could / May) his flight be late?
            1

Carla: Maybe, or he (could / may) be caught in traffic.
                          2

George: I don't think so. There isn't much traffic at this time.

Carla: There (might not / mightn't) be a lot of traffic, but perhaps he got lost on the way.
               3

George: (May / Could) we call him?
            4

Carla: I tried, but he didn't answer. His cell phone (might not / couldn't) be turned on.
                                                           5

George: Let's call the airline. They (may / might) have some information about the flight.
                                           6

Carla: Good idea. Oh! I see lights in the driveway. (Might / Could) that be his car?
                                                            7

14 Your Turn

Write two things you may/might (not) do for each of these times.

Example:
Tonight, I may do my homework, or I might call my parents.

1. Tonight, _____

2. This weekend, _____

3. Next year, _____

8e *Maybe* OR *May Be*

Antonio is thinking about a young woman he saw.
"**Maybe** she's not married," he thinks.

1. *Maybe* (one word) and *may be* (two words) both express possibility.

2. *Maybe* (one word) is an adverb. It comes in front of a subject and a verb. It means "perhaps" or "possibly."

    Maybe she's not married.

3. *May be* (two words) is used as the verb of a sentence.

    She **may be** married.

---

15 Practice

Antonio saw an attractive woman on the street yesterday. Her name is Angelica. Complete the sentences with *may be* or *maybe*.

1. Her name is Angelica. _____Maybe_____ she's French.

2. Or, she _____ Italian. He doesn't know.

3. He doesn't know what she does. _____ she's a dancer.

4. Yes, she _____ a ballet dancer.

5. He saw Angelica for the first time yesterday. Why didn't he see her before?

    _____ she doesn't live in this town.

6. Yes, she _____ from out of town.

7. He said, "Hello," and asked, "What's your name?" She didn't say anything. _____ she doesn't understand English.

8. At first Antonio thought, "She _____ from another country." So he said slowly, "My name is Antonio. What is your name?"

9. She looked at him. There was something in her eyes. _____ she thought he was impolite.

10. Then she said, "Angelica." _____ it wasn't her real name. Then she ran away.

16 What Do You Think?

Finish the story about Antonio and Angelica. Use *maybe* and *may be*.

17 What Do You Think?

Work in pairs or groups. Look at the two photos. Use *may, might,* or *maybe* to make guesses about what you think these objects are.

A.

1. _____

2. _____

3. _____

4. _____

B.

1. _____

2. _____

3. _____

4. _____

18 Your Turn

Say three good things and three bad things that may happen to you this year. Use *maybe* or *may be*.

Example:
Maybe I'll pass my English exam.
If I don't pass, I may be in the same class again!

8f Let's and Why Don't We to Make Suggestions; Why Don't You to Give Advice

Form / Function

SUGGESTIONS

1. We can make suggestions with *let's* and *why don't we* + a base verb. They have the same meaning.

2. *Let's* is a contraction of *let + us*. We usually say and write *let's*. *Let us* is very formal. We rarely use it.

3. *Let's* includes you and one or more other people.

AFFIRMATIVE				
Let's	Base Verb		Ways to Agree	Ways to Disagree
Let's	**watch**	TV.	Good idea. Sure. OK. Fine with me.	I'd rather not. Let's ... instead. Let's not.
	go	dancing.		
	eat	now.		

NEGATIVE				
Let's Not	Base Verb		Ways to Agree	Ways to Disagree
Let's not	**watch**	TV.	I agree. Good idea. Sure. OK.	Oh, I'd really like to. Why not?
	go	dancing.		
	eat	now.		

Why Don't We	Base Verb		Ways to Agree	Ways to Disagree
Why don't we	**watch**	TV?	Good idea. Sure. OK.	I'd rather not. Let's not. Let's ... instead.
	go	dancing?		
	eat	now?		

17

Modal Auxiliaries and Related Forms

ADVICE

4. We use *why don't you* + a base verb to give friendly advice to someone.

Why Don't You	Base Verb		Ways to Agree	Ways to Disagree
Why don't you	**rest**	a little?	Good idea. OK. I will.	I have no time. I'm OK.
	go	to the doctor?		
	take	an aspirin?		

19 Practice

Make suggestions with *let's* or *why don't we* and one of the ideas in the list or with your own ideas.

buy her a gift   hurry
go get a pizza   stay home and watch TV
go for a walk   study together in the library
go see it   watch it

1. It's a beautiful day.

   Why don't we go for a walk?

2. There's a good movie at the movie theater here.

   _____

3. It's raining again tonight. I don't want to go out. What should we do?

   _____

4. I'm hungry, but there's nothing to eat here.

   _____

5. There's a good football game on TV now.

   _____

6. It's Carol's birthday next Monday.

   _____

7. We have a test tomorrow.

   _____

8. Class starts in a few minutes.

   _____

20 Practice

Look at these problems. Give advice to your friend with *why don't you* and one of the ideas from the list, or use your own ideas.

ask her what she wants	call the store
go to the dentist	put on a sweater
have a cup of coffee	take an aspirin
have a piece of fruit	tell him/her what happened

1. Your friend: I can't find my credit card. I think I left it in the department store today.

   You: *Why don't you call the store?*

2. Your friend: I left my essay for my English class at home. My teacher wants it today.

   You: _____

3. Your friend: I have a terrible headache.

   You: _____

4. Your friend: I don't know what to get my mother for her birthday.

   You: _____

5. Your friend: I have a toothache.

   You: _____

6. Your friend: I'm cold.

   You: _____

7. Your friend: Reviewing for the test is making me sleepy.

   You: _____

8. Your friend: I'm hungry, but I don't have time to eat lunch right now.

   You: _____

21 Your Turn

Work with a partner or the class. Name three problems that you have.

Example:
You: I'm gaining weight.
Your partner: Why don't you eat less?

22 Your Turn

Make three suggestions for a place and time for a class party. Use *let's* or *why don't we*. Give answers.

Example:
You: Why don't we have the party in a hotel?
Your partner: No, that's too expensive.

8g *Should, Ought To,* and *Had Better* to Give Advice

I broke my friend's CD player.
Should I **buy** a new one for him?

ADVICE

AFFIRMATIVE STATEMENT			NEGATIVE STATEMENT		
Subject	Modal	Base Verb	Subject	Modal + *Not*	Base Verb
You	**should** **ought to**	**buy** a new one.	You	**should not** **shouldn't**	**lie** about it.

1. We use *should* and *ought to* + base verb to say what is the best or right thing to do. *Should* and *ought to* have the same meaning.

2. We usually do not use *ought to* in questions, negative sentences, and short answers. We use *should* instead.

   You **shouldn't stay** up late. You have an exam tomorrow.

   Should I **send** a card?
   Yes, you **should.**

STRONG ADVICE OR WARNING

AFFIRMATIVE STATEMENTS				NEGATIVE STATEMENTS		
Subject	Modal	Base Verb		Subject	Modal + *Not*	Base Verb
You	**had better**	**hurry.**		We	**had better not**	**wait.**
We	**'d better**	**eat**	now.	She	**'d better not**	**leave.**

3. We use *had better* to give a strong recommendation. *Had better* often suggests a warning and is stronger than *should* or *ought to*. The speaker expects the action to happen. The contraction of *had better* is *'d better*.

   It's raining. You **had better take** an umbrella.
   We**'d better not be** late or we'll miss the plane.

4. We rarely use *had better* in questions.

23 Practice

Say what Sandra should or should not do.

1. She doesn't do her homework.

She should do her homework.

2. She goes out with her friends every night.

_____

3. She never goes to the gym.

_____

4. She always eats out.

_____

5. She drinks a lot of coffee.

_____

6. She stays out at dance parties all night.

_____

7. She wears dirty shoes inside the house.

_____

8. She stays in bed until noon on weekends.

_____

9. She lends her car to her friends.

_____

10. She spends all her money on clothes and make-up.

_____

24 Practice

Benny is overweight and is not feeling well. He eats, smokes, and works too much. Use _had better_ or _had better not_ with the words in parentheses to give him strong advice.

1. (eat less) *You had better eat less.* _____

2. (drink a lot of soft drinks) _____

3. (drink too much coffee) _____

4. (get more exercise) _____

5. (use less salt) _____

6. (eat lots of snacks) _____

7. (work overtime often) _____

8. (see a doctor) _____

What Do You Think?

What is your advice for Benny?

Example:
He'd better lose some weight.

26 **Practice**

Give strong advice in these situations. Write a sentence with *had better* and a sentence with *had better not*.

1. I'm going out, and it's starting to rain.

   You had better take an umbrella.

   You'd better not go out.

2. I think I have a temperature.

   _____

   _____

3. I might miss an important interview. I have to be there in ten minutes.

   _____

   _____

4. I have to go by car, but there isn't much gas in it.

   _____

   _____

5. I am driving too fast. The speed limit is 40 miles an hour.

   _____

   _____

27 **Your Turn**

Say what you had better do to keep healthy. Say what you had better not do.

Example:
I'd better exercise more, and I'd better not smoke.

8h *Prefer ... to, Like ... Better Than,* and *Would Rather* to Express Preference

Form / Function

I **prefer** playing football **to** basketball.

1. We can use *prefer ... to* to express preferences. We can use a noun or a gerund as an object after *prefer*. (A gerund is a verb + *–ing* used as a noun.)

Subject	*Prefer*	Object	*To*	Object
I	**prefer**	football	**to**	basketball.
		playing football		playing basketball.

2. We can also use *like* with *better than* or other comparative forms to express preferences. We can use a noun or a gerund as an object after *like*.

Subject	*Like*	Object	Comparative Form	Object
I	**like**	football	**better than**	basketball.
		playing football		playing basketball.

3. We can also use *would rather (not)* to express preferences. We use *than* when we talk about two things.

Subject	*Would Rather (Not)*	Base Verb	Object	*Than*	Object
I	**would rather** **'d rather**	**play**	football	**than**	(play) basketball.
	would rather not* **'d rather not***	**play**	football.		

*We do not use the negative form *wouldn't* in sentences with *would rather + than*.

4. *Prefer ... to, like ... better,* and *would rather* have the same meaning. We use them to say what we prefer to do, or that we like one thing more than another.

> I **prefer** salad **to** soup.
> OR I **like** salad **better** than soup.
> OR I'**d rather** have salad than soup.

5. In questions with *would rather,* we often use *or.*

> Would you rather have salad **or** soup?

28 Practice

Complete the sentences with *than, to,* and *or.*

1. I'd rather sit by the window _____*than*_____ sit at the back of the restaurant.
2. I like the table by the window better _____ the table at the back.
3. I prefer the table by the window _____ the table at the back.
4. I like rice better _____ potatoes.
5. I prefer rice _____ potatoes.
6. I'd rather have rice _____ potatoes.
7. Would you rather have fish _____ meat?
8. I prefer having fish _____ having meat.
9. Do you like eating fish better _____ eating meat?
10. Would you rather pay cash _____ pay with a credit card?
11. I prefer paying with a credit card _____ paying cash.
12. I like paying by credit card better _____ paying cash.

29 Practice

Write sentences with *I'd rather* or *I prefer* and one of the items from the list.

eat later	go now	phone them
go by plane	go to a restaurant	stand
take a taxi	watch a video	

1. Let's take the bus.

    (prefer) *I prefer taking a taxi.*

2. Would you like to sit down?

    (rather) _____

3. Shall we eat at home?

(prefer) _____

4. Do you want to watch TV?

(rather) _____

5. Shall we drive there?

(prefer) _____

6. Would you like to write a thank you card?

(rather) _____

7. Do you want to stay a few more minutes?

(prefer) _____

8. Would you like to eat now?

(prefer) _____

30 Your Turn

What would you rather do? Use *I'd rather* to write what you prefer.

Example:
play football or soccer
I'd rather play soccer than football.

1. play football or soccer

_____

2. live in the country or the city

_____

3. be married or be single

_____

4. drink tea or coffee

_____

5. do homework or watch TV

_____

8i *Have To, Have Got To,* and *Must* to Express Necessity

She **doesn't have to work** today.

HAVE TO: PRESENT AND FUTURE

AFFIRMATIVE STATEMENTS			NEGATIVE STATEMENTS		
Subject	*Have/Has To*	Base Verb	Subject	*Not Have To*	Base Verb
I	**have to***		I	**do not have to**	
You			You	**don't have to**	
He/She/It	**has to***	**work.**	He/She/It	**does not have to** / **doesn't have to**	**work.**
We	**have to***		We	**do not have to**	
They			They	**don't have to**	

*We do not contract *have to* and *has to* with the subject.

CORRECT: I have to work.
INCORRECT: I~~'ve~~ to work.

YES/NO QUESTIONS				SHORT ANSWERS	
Do/Does	Subject	*Have To*	Base Verb	Yes,	No,
Do	I	**have to**	**work?**	you **do.**	you **don't.**
	you			I/we **do.**	I/we **don't.**
Does	he/she/it			he/she/it **does.**	he/she/it **doesn't.**
Do	we			you **do.**	you **don't.**
	they			they **do.**	they **don't.**

26

Unit 8

HAVE TO: PAST

AFFIRMATIVE STATEMENTS			NEGATIVE STATEMENTS		
Subject	*Had To*	Base Verb	Subject	*Not Have To*	Base Verb
I You He/She/It We They	**had to***	**work.**	I You He/She/It We They	**did not have to** **didn't have to**	**work.**

*We do not contract *had to* with the subject.

CORRECT: I had to work.
INCORRECT: ~~I'd~~ to work.

YES/NO QUESTIONS				SHORT ANSWERS	
Did	Subject	*Have To*	Base Verb	Yes,	No,
Did	I you he/she/it we they	**have to**	**work?**	you **did.** I/we **did.** he/she/it **did.** you **did.** they **did.**	you **didn't.** I/we **didn't.** he/she/it **didn't.** you **didn't.** they **didn't.**

HAVE GOT TO: PRESENT AND FUTURE

Subject	*Have/Has Got To*	Base Verb	
I You	**have got to** **'ve got to**	**work**	now. later. tomorrow.
He/She/It	**has got to** **'s got to**		
We They	**have got to** **'ve got to**		

MUST: PRESENT AND FUTURE

Subject	Modal	Base Verb	
I You He/She/It We They	**must**	**work**	now. tonight. next week.

1. *Must, have to,* and *have got to* have almost the same meaning. They all mean that it is necessary to do something.

2. *Must* is the strongest form. We use *must* in requirements, rules, and laws. We often use *must* in written instructions.

> You **must take** an entrance exam. (School requirements)
> Drivers **must signal** before they turn right or left. (Driver's manual)

3. When *must* expresses necessity, we use it only to refer to the present or the future. To refer to the past, we use *had to.*

> CORRECT: I had to work last Saturday.
> INCORRECT: I ~~must work~~ last Saturday.

4. We usually use *have to* and *have got to* in everyday conversation. *Have to* and *have got to* have the same meaning.

> It's Saturday, but I **have to work.**
> It's Saturday, but I**'ve got to work.**
> I **had to work** last Saturday, too.

5. We do not usually use *have got to* in questions and negative statements.

6. We use *have got to* only to refer to present and future necessity. To refer to the past, we use *had to.*

> CORRECT: We had to finish this homework.
> INCORRECT: We ~~had got to~~ finish this homework.

---

31 Practice

Change the written information with *must* to a spoken form with *have to* or *have got to.*

1. All students must register and pay fees.

   All students have to register and pay fees.

2. All students must register before taking courses.

   _____

3. Every student must take an English placement exam.

   _____

4. Every new student must attend orientation during registration week.

   _____

5. Students must apply for parking permits during registration.

_____

6. Students must present registration forms on the first day of classes.

_____

32 Practice

This is Mr. Krone and his two children, Bill and Jane. What do they have to do every day?

	Mr. Krone	Bill and Jane
Get up	7:00	7:30
Leave home	7:30	8:00
Be at the office	8:30	—
Be at school	—	8:30
Go to bed	11:30	10:00

1. Mr. Krone _____ *has to* _____ get up at 7:00 in the morning to go to work.

2. Bill and Jane _____ get up at 7:30 to go to school.

3. Mr. Krone _____ leave home at 7:30 in the morning to go to work.

4. Bill and Jane _____ leave home at 8:00 to go to school.

5. Bill and Jane _____ be at school at 8:30.

6. Mr. Krone _____ be at the office at 8:30.

7. Mr. Krone _____ go to bed at 11:30 in the evening because he is always very tired.

8. Bill and Jane _____ go to bed at 10:00.

A. Mr. Krone had a busy week. Match each situation with what he had to do.

Situations   **He had to ...**

_____ **1.** He got sick.   **a.** work overtime

_____ **2.** He had a lot of work.   **b.** take it to the mechanic

_____ **3.** His car broke down.   **c.** write a big check

_____ **4.** His taxes were due.   **d.** go to the doctor

_____ **5.** Mrs. Krone was traveling.   **e.** rest

_____ **6.** He got very tired.   **f.** do all the cooking

B. Now write a sentence with *had to* for each solution.

1. _He had to go to the doctor because he got sick._ ____

2. _____

3. _____

4. _____

5. _____

6. _____

|34| Practice

Work with a partner. Write questions about what Mr. Krone had to do last week.

1. A: _Did Mr. Krone have to go to the dentist?_ ____

   B: No, he didn't.

2. A: _____

   B: No, he didn't.

3. A: _____

   B: Yes, he did.

4. A: _____

   B: No, he didn't.

5. A: _____

   B: Yes, he did.

6. A: _____

   B: No, he didn't.

35 Practice

Underline the correct form in parentheses. If both forms are correct, underline both of them.

1. Bonnie (<u>has to</u> / <u>has got to</u>) travel to Seoul, Korea next month.

1
2. She doesn't have a passport, so she (had to / had got to) apply for one last week.

2
3. Before she applied for her new passport, she (must / had to) have her picture taken.

3
4. When she gets to Seoul, she (must / has got to) visit many customers.

4
5. The director of her company in Korea (has to / must) introduce her to them.

5
6. When she returns home, she (must / had to) write letters to everyone she met in Seoul.

6

36 Your Turn

Write three things you had to do last week and three things you have to/have got to do this week.

Example:
Last week, I had to do my laundry. This week, I've got to write an important essay.

8j Must Not to Forbid and Not Have To to Express Lack of Necessity

Form / Function

Look at the sign!
We **mustn't swim** here.

1. We use *must not* + a base verb to say that something is not allowed or is forbidden. *Must not* is stronger than *should not*.

Subject	Modal + *Not*	Base Verb
I You He/She/It We They	**must not** **mustn't**	**park** here.

2. We use *not have to* to show that something is not necessary. (See page 26 for the forms of *not have to*.)

   Tomorrow is Sunday. You **don't have to** get up early.
   I **had to** get up early yesterday.

37 Practice

Look at the following instructions about flights and planes. Then write sentences with *mustn't* or *don't have to*.

1. It isn't necessary for you to fasten your seat belt all through a flight, but it's a good idea.
   You don't have to fasten your seat belt all through a flight.

2. It is forbidden to smoke on the aircraft.
   You must not smoke on the aircraft.

3. It isn't necessary for you to carry your medications with you, but it's a good idea.
   _____

4. It isn't necessary for you to put labels on your luggage, but it's a good idea in case it gets lost.
   _____

5. It is forbidden to carry knives or sharp objects in your carry-on luggage.
   _____

6. It is forbidden to carry more than two pieces of carry-on luggage.
   _____

7. It isn't necessary to carry breakable objects in your carry-on luggage, but if you don't, they might get broken.
   _____

8. It isn't necessary for you to stay in your seat all through the flight.
   _____

9. It is forbidden to leave your luggage unattended.
   _____

10. It is forbidden to take items from strangers on the aircraft.

_____

11. It isn't necessary to eat light meals, but you might feel better if you do.

_____

12. It is forbidden to take fruits and other foods from one country to another.

_____

38 Practice

Look at these washing labels on clothes. Say what they mean. Use _must, must not,_ or _don't have to._

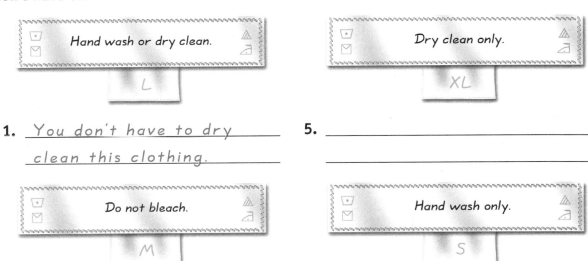

1. _You don't have to dry_
   clean this clothing.

5. _____

_____

2. _____

_____

6. _____

_____

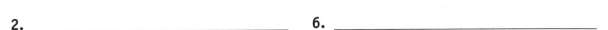

3. _____

_____

7. _____

_____

4. _____

_____

8. _____

_____

Modal Auxiliaries and Related Forms

39 Practice

You are going for a vacation in the sun in the Caribbean. You will be staying at a nice hotel. What mustn't you forget? What do you not have to take?

1. blankets
2. a coat
3. gloves
4. a grammar book
5. knives and forks
6. my passport
7. my plane tickets
8. a suit
9. my sunglasses
10. a swimsuit

1. *I don't have to take blankets.* _____

2. _____

3. _____

4. _____

5. _____

6. *I mustn't forget my passport.* _____

7. _____

8. _____

9. _____

10. _____

40 Your Turn

You are going for a weekend at a friend's house. Write three things you mustn't forget to take with you and three things you don't have to take.

Example:
I mustn't forget my toothbrush.

Things I mustn't forget

1. _____

2. _____

3. _____

Things I don't have to take

1. _____

2. _____

3. _____

8k *Must* to Make Deductions

A: Who is that woman? Is she a student?
B: I don't know, but I've seen her go into the teachers' room.
A: Oh. She **must be** a teacher. She **must not be** a student.

1. We use *must* for deductions, or guesses, from facts that we know. *Must* expresses what is logical in the situation.

   Fact: Tony has three houses and four cars.
   Deduction: He **must** be rich.

2. We use *must not* for a negative deduction.

   Fact: Tony has three companies. He works very hard.
   Deduction: He **must not** have a lot of free time.

3. Remember, we also use *must* to express strong necessity, and we use *must not* when we forbid something.

   You **must** do your homework.
   You **must not** drive when the traffic light is red.

Three people are having breakfast in a hotel. Some of their belongings are on their tables. What can you tell about their owners? Complete the sentences with *must*.

A.

1. The owner _____ *must be a woman.*

2. The owner _____

3. The owner _____

B.

1. The owner _____

2. The owner _____

3. The owner _____

C.

1. The owner _____

2. The owner _____

3. The owner _____

Your Turn

Work with a partner. Look at the photos of the two people. Make deductions based on what you see in the photos. Make three sentences for each photo using *must* or *must not.*

Example:
He must be a doctor.
She must be a photographer.

81 Imperatives

Form

1. We use the base form of the verb in imperative sentences. The verb is always the same form.

2. We use the imperative to address one or more people. The subject of the sentence, *you,* is understood. It is not stated.

   Open the window.

3. We can use **please** at the beginning or at the end of the sentence. At the end of the sentence, it must follow a comma.

   Please open your books.
   Open your books, **please.**

4. For the negative, we use *do not* or *don't* before the base form of the verb.

   Do not enter.
   Don't be late!

We use the imperative to tell someone to do something. Imperatives are used for these purposes.

Function	Example
1. Commands	**Wash** your hands.
2. Requests	Please **turn off** the lights.
3. Directions	**Turn** right at the traffic light.
4. Instructions	**Cook** for 15 minutes.
5. Warnings	**Be** careful.
6. Advice	**Get** some sleep.

43 Practice

Complete the teacher's instructions with verbs in the list. Use *don't* where necessary.

be	close	make	sit	talk
chew	do	open	stop	work

1. _Close_ your books.

2. _____ to your neighbor in class.

3. _____ gum in class.

4. _____ sentences with these words.

5. _____ your books to page 210.

6. _____ with your partner.

7. _____ homework in class.

8. _____ quiet!

9. _____ down.

10. _____ that noise!

Add two more of your own.

11. _____

12. _____

44 Practice

Work with a partner. Give advice to a friend in these situations. Use affirmative and negative imperatives.

1. I have a cold.

Don't go to school. Stay home and rest. Drink lots of tea with lemon.

_____

2. I can't fall asleep at night.

_____

_____

3. My computer won't start.

_____

_____

4. My grades are bad.

_____

_____

5. I can't save money.

_____

_____

45 Your Turn

Give instructions. You are going on a long vacation. Your friend is coming to your home every day to take care of things. Make a list of six things for your friend to do.

THINGS TO DO

1. *Take the mail in.* _____

2. _____

3. _____

4. _____

5. _____

6. _____

Modal Auxiliaries and Related Forms

WRITING: Write a Friendly Letter

Write a letter to a friend about changes in your life.

Step 1. Read the situation.

You have been accepted at a famous university to study for your Bachelor of Arts degree. The university is famous, but it is not in your city. You have to leave home and move far away. You are writing a letter to a friend explaining the changes in your life.

Step 2. Think about these facts and write sentences using modals.

1. move to a new city or country
2. make new friends
3. live in the school dorm or find a cheap apartment
4. leave things behind
5. not come home for long periods

Step 3. Rewrite the sentences as a paragraph as in the model letter below. For more writing guidelines, see pages 216–220.

> May 1, 20XX
>
> Dear Paul,
>   I'm writing to tell you that I got accepted at the University of
> _____. It's a famous university, but it is not in my city, so I have
> to go live there. I'm going next month. I have to do many things.
>
>
>
>
>   Your friend,

Step 4. Evaluate your paragraph.

Checklist

_____ Did you write the letter in correct letter form?
_____ Did you indent your paragraph?
_____ Did you use some modal auxiliaries in your sentences?

Step 5. Work with a partner to edit your paragraph. Check spelling, punctuation, and grammar.

Step 6. Write a final copy of your paragraph.

40

SELF-TEST

A **Choose the best answer, A, B, C, or D, to complete the sentence. Mark your answer by darkening the oval with the same letter.**

1. You _____ put that blouse in the washing machine. It says dry clean only.

   A. must   Ⓐ Ⓑ Ⓒ Ⓓ
   B. mustn't
   C. don't have to
   D. have to

2. I _____ read until I was six.

   A. can't   Ⓐ Ⓑ Ⓒ Ⓓ
   B. shouldn't
   C. couldn't
   D. mustn't

3. _____ I borrow your pen, please?

   A. May   Ⓐ Ⓑ Ⓒ Ⓓ
   B. Would
   C. Should
   D. Will

4. I _____ go to the market. I need some eggs for this cake.

   A. might   Ⓐ Ⓑ Ⓒ Ⓓ
   B. could
   C. must
   D. mustn't

5. We _____ leave now. It's getting late.

   A. could   Ⓐ Ⓑ Ⓒ Ⓓ
   B. should
   C. might
   D. are able to

6. Sam: What should we have for lunch?
   Kate: _____ pizza?

   A. Why don't we have   Ⓐ Ⓑ Ⓒ Ⓓ
   B. I'd rather have
   C. We'd better have
   D. We have to have

7. _____ you open the door for me, please?

   A. May   Ⓐ Ⓑ Ⓒ Ⓓ
   B. Could
   C. Should
   D. Might

8. I'm sorry, I _____ to play football with you next week. I'm going out of town.

   A. can't   Ⓐ Ⓑ Ⓒ Ⓓ
   B. don't have
   C. won't be able
   D. must not

9. I don't know her. She _____ a student.

   A. maybe   Ⓐ Ⓑ Ⓒ Ⓓ
   B. may be
   C. 'd rather be
   D. should

10. _____ You are going to fall.

    A. You may be careful.   Ⓐ Ⓑ Ⓒ Ⓓ
    B. You could be careful.
    C. You are careful!
    D. Be careful!

Modal Auxiliaries and Related Forms

B Find the underlined word or phrase, A, B, C, or D, that is incorrect. Mark your answer by darkening the oval with the same letter.

1. You <u>don't</u> <u>have be</u> <u>a</u> citizen <u>to get</u> a
       A   B   C   D
   driver's license.

   Ⓐ Ⓑ Ⓒ Ⓓ

2. <u>You</u> must <u>to drive</u> with a seatbelt <u>in</u> this
    A   B C   D
   country.

   Ⓐ Ⓑ Ⓒ Ⓓ

3. In most <u>movie theaters</u>, senior citizens
             A
   <u>can't</u> <u>have to</u> pay full price for <u>a movie</u>.
    B   C   D

   Ⓐ Ⓑ Ⓒ Ⓓ

4. The store <u>maybe</u> very <u>crowded</u> tomorrow
             A   B
   because <u>there is</u> <u>a</u> big sale.
           C   D

   Ⓐ Ⓑ Ⓒ Ⓓ

5. You <u>could</u> not <u>sign</u> <u>anything</u> before
       A   B   C
   reading <u>it</u> carefully.
         D

   Ⓐ Ⓑ Ⓒ Ⓓ

6. <u>Would</u> you <u>rather see</u> a movie <u>to</u> stay at
    A   B   C
   home and <u>watch</u> a video?
            D

   Ⓐ Ⓑ Ⓒ Ⓓ

7. <u>You better</u> <u>study</u> more, or you <u>might</u> not
    A   B   C
   <u>pass</u> the class.
    D

   Ⓐ Ⓑ Ⓒ Ⓓ

8. Karen <u>was</u> able <u>change</u> <u>the</u> flat tire
        A   B   C
   <u>by herself</u> yesterday.
    D

   Ⓐ Ⓑ Ⓒ Ⓓ

9. You <u>mightn't</u> try <u>to take</u> the entrance
        A   B
   exam without <u>preparing</u> for <u>it</u> first.
                C   D

   Ⓐ Ⓑ Ⓒ Ⓓ

10. We <u>must</u> to work overtime last week
        A
    <u>in order to</u> <u>finish</u> <u>the project</u> by the
        B   C   D
    deadline.

    Ⓐ Ⓑ Ⓒ Ⓓ

UNIT 9

GERUNDS AND INFINITIVES

9a Gerund as Subject and Object

Climbing rocks is dangerous.
Melanie loves **climbing** rocks.

1. To form a gerund, we add –*ing* to the base form of the verb. See page 215 for spelling rules for adding –*ing* to the base form of verbs.

Base Verb	Gerund
climb	**climbing**
go	**going**
run	**running**
watch	**watching**

2. We can use a gerund like a noun. It can be the subject or the object of a sentence.

Subject	Verb	Object
Climbing rocks	takes	a lot of energy.

Subject	Verb	Object
Melanie	loves	**climbing** rocks.

3. We can use a gerund as the subject of a question.

   Is **climbing** rocks dangerous?

1 Practice

Complete the sentences with the gerund form of the verbs in the list. You may use a verb more than one time.

drive	fly	sleep	watch
fish	play	wash	

1. _Flying_ in an airplane is not really dangerous.
2. John is afraid of _____ in an airplane. He travels by car.
3. He loves his car and enjoys _____ it.
4. On Sundays, his favorite pastime is _____ his car.
5. _____ football is too tiring for John.
6. He prefers _____ football on television.
7. His favorite sport is _____ in a river.
8. _____ in a river is relaxing for John.
9. He likes _____ his dirty clothes in the washing machine.
10. John also likes _____ late on Sundays.

2 Practice

Say which activities in the list are easy and which are difficult for you. Use gerunds in your answers.

Example:
I think cooking is difficult.

cook	ride a horse	ski	write letters
dance	run	swim	
learn English	sing	water ski	
read	skate	windsurf	

3 Your Turn

Say five things that you like or that you think are fun.

Example:
Dancing is fun.
I love listening to music.

9b Verb + Gerund

We **enjoy skiing** in the mountains. Little Jamie came with us this year.

1. We can use a gerund as the object of certain verbs. Here are some of the verbs.

consider	finish	keep on	quit
discuss	give up	not mind	start
dislike	imagine	postpone	stop
enjoy	keep	put off	think about

2. We use a gerund after the verb *go* for some activities.

go **bowling**	go **dancing**	go **jogging**	go **shopping**
go **camping**	go **fishing**	go **running**	go **sightseeing**
go **climbing**	go **hiking**	go **sailing**	go **swimming**

Practice

Complete the sentences with the gerund form of the verb in parentheses.

1. After Mike stopped (work) _____ *working* _____, he went

   (bowl) _____ with his friends.

2. Ted was considering (visit) _____ his sister next week, but he

   postponed (go) _____ for another two weeks.

3. It didn't stop (rain) _____, so we put off (go) _____

   until later.

4. Timmy quit (watch) _____ cartoons when he started

   (go) _____ to school.

5. My parents keep (tell) _____ me rock climbing is dangerous, but it's

   hard to give up (do) _____ something I enjoy.

6. I enjoy (receive) _____ letters, but I always put off

   (reply) _____ to them.

7. We postponed (go) _____ on the trip until next weekend.

8. I don't mind (go) _____ sightseeing, but we must go

   (shop) _____ later.

9. He finished (do) _____ his homework, and then he went

   (jog) _____.

10. I gave up (fix) _____ my car, and I am considering

    (buy) _____ a new one.

5 Your Turn

Complete the chart with two things you enjoy doing, dislike doing, and don't mind
doing. Then ask two classmates about themselves and complete the chart.

Example:
I enjoy going to the movies. I dislike cleaning the house, but I don't mind cooking.

Student	Enjoy Doing	Dislike Doing	Don't Mind Doing
1. Me			
2.			
3.			

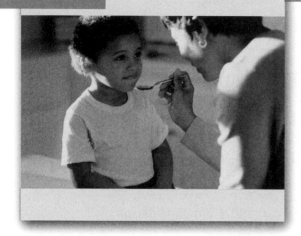

6 | Your Turn

What do you like to do for fun? Write three things with *go* **+ a gerund.**

Example:
I like going shopping. I also like going fishing and bowling.

1. _____

2. _____

3. _____

9c Verb + Infinitive

Form / Function

She **tried to give** him his medicine, but he **refused to open** his mouth.

We use an infinitive (*to* + the base form of a verb) after certain verbs. Here are some of the verbs.

agree	expect	manage	pretend	would like
appear	forget	mean	promise	would love
can't afford	hope	need	refuse	would prefer
can't wait	intend	offer	try	
decide	learn	plan	want	

Complete the sentences with the infinitive form of the verbs in the list.

A.

be   break in   catch   get into   steal

Someone tried ___*to break in*___ to my office last week. He planned
1
_____ some of my files. He managed _____
2   3
the building. He passed by the security officer. He pretended _____ an
4
electrician. When the security officer tried _____ him, he ran away.
5

B.

ask   go   take   visit

I have an old friend in Montreal, Canada. I promised _____ her. I'm
1
planning _____ in November. I wanted _____ you about
2   3
the weather. Do I need _____ a heavy coat with me?
4

C.

find   give   quit   take care of

My company refused _____ me a week off. I need
1
_____ my sick mother. So I decided _____ my job. I'll try
2   3
_____ another job later.
4

D.

build   buy   do   finish   fix

We can't afford _____ a new house, so we decided
1
_____ this one up. For example, we need _____ another
2   3
bathroom. I have learned _____ the plumbing, and I plan
4
_____ the new bathroom next month.
5

E.

drive   fix   pay

I can't wait _____ my new car on the highway. I can't afford
                          1

_____ a mechanic to repair it when it breaks down, so I will learn
        2

how _____ it myself.
        3

9d Verb + Gerund or Infinitive

Oli **loves waterskiing.**
He **loves to waterski** in Hawaii.

We can use a gerund or an infinitive after certain verbs. The meaning is the same.
Here are some examples.

like	hate	can't stand	continue
love	begin	start	try

Practice

Complete the sentences with a gerund and an infinitive of each of the verbs given.

1. do

Ted hates _____*doing*_____ his homework.

Ted hates _____*to do*_____ his homework.

2. sit

He likes _____ in front of the television.

He likes _____ in front of the television.

3. argue

He doesn't like _____

He doesn't like _____

4. wait

He can't stand _____ in long lines.

He can't stand _____ in long lines.

5. go out

He loves _____ with his friends on weekends.

He loves _____ with his friends on weekends.

9 Your Turn

Use the sentences in Practice 8 to make statements about yourself. They don't have to be true.

Example:
I like doing my homework.

10 Practice

Complete the sentences with the gerund or the infinitive of the verbs in parentheses. Sometimes two answers are possible.

A.

Gary is learning (play) _____*to play*_____ the guitar. He wants
                              1

(write) _____ his own music, and he hopes (become) _____
              2   3

a famous guitarist one day. He would like (make) _____ a lot of money
                                                              4

and travel around the world.

B.

Janet would like (be) _____ an artist because she loves

1

(draw) _____ . She has decided (go) _____ to art school

2   3

next year. A famous art school in New York agreed (give) _____ her a

4

scholarship. Without it, she could not afford (go) _____ .

5

C.

Amy wants (become) _____ an actress. Her parents would like her

1

(go) _____ to college and become a dentist. She refuses

2

(listen) _____ to their advice and plans (go) _____

3   4

to Los Angeles next year.

D.

Tony doesn't like (study) _____ . He loves (repair) _____

1   2

all kinds of things, but he prefers (repair) _____ cars. He wants

3

(be) _____ a mechanic. He hopes (have) _____ his own

4   5

garage one day.

II Practice

Complete the sentences with the infinitive or gerund form of the verb in parentheses.

A.

Kate and Ben can't afford (go) _____*to go*_____ on vacation this year, but they

1

intend (save) _____ enough money to travel to Europe next year. They

2

would like (visit) _____ three or four countries. They are really looking

3

forward to (go) _____ .

4

B.

Michael hates (clean) _____ his apartment. He would like

(have) _____ someone clean it for him, but he can't afford

(pay) _____ them. He manages (do) _____

some cleaning before people come to visit. Usually he puts off (clean) _____

until the last day or hour.

12 Your Turn

Write 10 sentences about your friends or family members. Use the verbs from List 1
followed by a gerund or an infinitive. You can use the ideas in List 2, or you can use
your own ideas.

Example:
My sister likes sewing.
My friend Charles loves playing chess.

List 1

dislike	enjoy	like	love	not mind

List 2

cook	listen to rock music	ride motorcycles
dance	play chess	sew
eat healthy food	play sports	stay out late with friends
exercise	read about philosophy	watch soap operas

1. _____

2. _____

3. _____

4. _____

5. _____

6. _____

7. _____

8. _____

9. _____

10. _____

9e Preposition + Gerund

Ken is good **at** skateboarding.

1. We can use a gerund after a preposition. The gerund is the object of the preposition.

    I apologize **for being** late.

2. Prepositions can follow certain verbs and adjectives.

Prepositions Following Verbs		Prepositions Following Adjectives	
apologize **for**	insist **on**	capable **of**	interested **in**
approve **of**	succeed **in**	excited **about**	pleased **about**
believe **in**	think **about**	fond **of**	tired **of**
care **about**	worry **about**	good **at**	sad **about**

    I am **thinking about** leaving early today. (verb + preposition)
    He is **good at** skateboarding. (adjective + preposition)

13 Practice

Complete the conversation with the gerund form of the verb in parentheses.

Tony: I'm tired of (do) _____*doing*_____ the same thing every day.
1

Ken: Well, what are you good at?

Tony: I'm good at (skateboard) _____ and (surf) _____.
2   3

I dream about (go) _____ to Hawaii one day.
4

Ken: Can't you think of (do) _____ anything else?
5

Tony: I have always been interested in (write) _____ for a newspaper.
6

I have often thought of (be) _____ a journalist. I'm not afraid
7

of (go) _____ to dangerous places.
8

Ken: But it's hard work!

Tony: I don't care about (work) _____ hard as long as I enjoy it. I don't
9

even care if I don't get paid for (do) _____ it.
10

14 Your Turn

Complete the sentences about yourself. Then tell a partner about yourself.

Example:
I'm good at swimming.

I'm good at _____

I'm not very good at _____, but I'm excellent at

_____

I'm interested in _____

I believe in _____

I look forward to _____

9f Infinitive of Purpose

We hold our nose **to show** that something smells bad.

We put a finger to our mouth **to ask** for quiet.

We cross our middle and index fingers **to wish** good luck.

1. We use an infinitive to talk about the reason or purpose for doing something (why someone does something).

> I went to the cafeteria **to have** some lunch.
> He's going to the supermarket **to buy** groceries.

2. In more formal English, we use *in order to*.

   She left early **in order to avoid** the heavy traffic.
   We're saving money **in order to buy** a new car.

3. We can also use *for* to show purpose. We use a noun after *for*.
   I went to the cafeteria **for** lunch.
   He's going to the supermarket **for** milk and bread.

15 | Practice

Where did you go yesterday? Why did you go to these places?

A. Match the words in column A with those in column B.

A	B
_f_ **1.** buy	**a.** a car
_____ **2.** cash	**b.** a check
_____ **3.** eat	**c.** a flight
_____ **4.** learn	**d.** lunch
_____ **5.** mail	**e.** some letters
_____ **6.** rent	**f.** some clothes
_____ **7.** reserve	**g.** Spanish

B. Use the phrases in part A to write sentences about the following places.

1. the post office

   I went to the post office to mail some letters.

2. the department store

   _____

3. the bank

   _____

4. the travel agency

   _____

5. a fast food restaurant

_____

6. a car rental agency

_____

7. night school

_____

16 Practice

Complete the sentences with _to_ or _for_.

1. I go to school _____*to*_____ learn English.

2. We go to school _____ get an education.

3. Some people need English _____ get a better job.

4. We need a grammar book _____ learn the rules.

5. We need a dictionary _____ vocabulary.

6. We use the Internet _____ do research.

7. I sometimes use my computer _____ do homework.

8. Our teacher sometimes uses videos _____ discussion.

9. Our teacher always gives us lots of exercises _____ homework.

10. We always have a lot of homework _____ do.

11. The library is a good place _____ do research.

12. It has computers _____ Internet searches.

17 Your Turn

Say why you do these things. Use _for_ or _to_ in your answers.

Example:
go on vacation
I go on vacation to relax and for fun.

go on vacation   play sports   work
go to school   save money

A. Match the ideas in column A with those in column B.

A	B
_b_ **1.** He's studying hard	**a.** keep in shape
_____ **2.** She's exercising	**b.** pass the test
_____ **3.** I turned up the volume	**c.** get there by tomorrow
_____ **4.** We must drive all night	**d.** hear the news better
_____ **5.** He must save money	**e.** study for the test
_____ **6.** We're going to the library	**f.** buy a motorbike

B. Use *in order to* to write sentences with the phrases in Part A.

1. _He's studying hard in order to pass the test._

2. _____

3. _____

4. _____

5. _____

6. _____

19 Your Turn

Complete the sentences to explain the meaning of some gestures in your country or culture.

1. _We kiss both cheeks_ _____ to say hello to a friend.

2. _____ to say goodbye to a friend.

3. _____ to say something is good.

4. _____ to say something is bad.

5. _____ to say someone is crazy.

9g Adjective + Infinitive

We were **amazed to see** a man walking in space.

1. We can use an infinitive after certain adjectives. Here are some of the adjectives.

afraid	frightened	sad
difficult	glad	safe
disappointed	happy	sorry
easy	pleased	surprised
foolish	right	wrong

I am **pleased to see** you.
She was **surprised to get** a letter.

2. We can also use adjectives with infinitives after **it.**

It is **difficult to speak** English.
It is **important to finish** on time.

20 Practice

Complete the sentences with the infinitive of the verbs in the list.

eat	get off	travel
fasten	get on	watch
find	have	
fly	learn	

1. People say it's dangerous _____to fly_____ on a plane.

2. I wasn't afraid _____ by plane.

3. Then I was disappointed _____ that the flight was delayed.

4. I was the first _____ the plane.

5. I was the last _____ the plane when it landed.

6. I was surprised _____ such tasty food.

7. It was necessary _____ the seat belt for take off and landing.

8. I was glad _____ a movie on the flight.

9. I was happy _____ my feet on the ground again.

10. I was pleased _____ my friends waiting for me.

21 Practice

Rewrite the sentences using *it* and an infinitive.

1. Learning to use a computer is easy.

   It is easy to learn to use a computer.

2. Being polite to customers is important.

   _____

3. Making mistakes when you speak English is normal.

   _____

4. Traveling to new countries is interesting.

   _____

5. Meeting people is fun.

   _____

6. Living in Tokyo is expensive.

   _____

7. Being on time is essential.

   _____

8. Waiting for more than 10 minutes is unusual here.

_____

9. Picking up a poisonous snake is dangerous.

_____

10. Taking tests is necessary.

_____

9h   *Enough* and *Too* with Adjectives and Adverbs; *Enough* and *Too* with Infinitives; *Enough* with Nouns

He is not **big enough** to wear the suit.
The suit is **too big** for him to wear.

1. We use *enough* after adjectives and adverbs but before nouns. *Enough* means that there is the right amount of something—not too much and not too little.

ADJECTIVE/ADVERB + *ENOUGH*			
Subject	Verb	Adjective/Adverb + *Enough*	Infinitive
She	isn't	old **enough**	to drive.
It	is	warm **enough**	to swim.
He	swims	fast **enough**	to win the race.

ENOUGH + NOUN			
Subject	Verb	*Enough* + Noun	Infinitive
I	have	**enough** eggs	to make an omelet.
He	has	**enough** money	to buy a CD.

2. We use *too* before adjectives and adverbs. *Too* means "more than enough."			

Subject	Verb	*Too* + Adjective/Adverb	Infinitive
I	am	**too** tired	to go out.
He	writes	**too** well	to fail the test.

22 Practice

Can you do these things? Answer each question with *too* or *enough*. You may use the adjectives in the list in your answers.

big	fast	rich	slow	tall
brave	funny	serious	small	weak
dangerous	poor	short	strong	

1. Can you touch the ceiling?

No, I can't. I'm not tall enough to reach the ceiling. OR I'm too short to reach the ceiling.

2. Can you carry a 60-pound suitcase?

_____

_____

3. Can you make people laugh?

_____

_____

4. Can you jump from an airplane?

_____

_____

5. Can you run a mile in one minute?

_____

_____

6. Can you put a whole apple in your mouth at one time?

_____

_____

7. Can you buy a palace?

_____

_____

Complete the sentences with *too* or *enough*.

1. I got up _____*too*_____ late this morning.

2. I ran to the bus stop, but I wasn't fast _____ to catch the bus.

3. At work, I had a client who talked _____ much.

4. I wanted to see my boss, but he didn't have _____ time to talk to me.

5. The day was _____ long.

9i   *Be Used To* + Gerund and *Be Accustomed To* + Gerund

Form / Function

I'm **not used to eating** this kind of food. I'm also **not accustomed to eating** with chopsticks. I'm **used to eating** with a knife and fork.

1. We use *be used to* + gerund or *be accustomed to* + gerund to talk about something that we are familiar with because we have done it often. *Be used to* and *be accustomed to* have the same meaning.

   I **am used to eating** with chopsticks.
   I **am accustomed to eating** with chopsticks.

2. Do not confuse *be used to* + gerund with *used to* + base verb. We use *used to* + base verb to talk about something that happened or was true in the past, but it is different or not true now.

   I **used to eat** with chopsticks when I lived in Japan. (Now I don't.)

24 Practice

Complete the sentences with *be used to* or *used to* plus the verbs in parentheses.

1. I (write) _____ *used to write* _____ on a typewriter many years ago. Now I write on a computer. At first it was hard, but now I (write) _____ *am used to writing* _____ on my computer and can't live without it.

2. My brother (live) _____ in London, but now he lives in New York. It was strange for him at first, but now he (live) _____ in New York, and he loves the lifestyle.

3. I have to be at work at 7:00 every morning, so I (go) _____ to bed early. I'm (not/go) _____ to bed late.

4. Before I got this job, I used to get up late. Now I have to be at work at 8:00 in the morning. It was difficult, but now I (get) _____ up early.

5. Yukio didn't like American food when he first arrived, but now he (eat) _____ it.

6. I am getting up at 6:00 tomorrow morning to go to the airport. I (not/get up) _____ early. I (get up) _____ at around 8:00.

7. Suzy found Japan strange at first. For example, she (not/take off) _____ her shoes before going into a house.

8. For six months after I bought the car, I (not/drive) _____ it much, but now I (drive) _____ it, and I love it.

Work with a partner. Ask and answer questions with *be used to* or *be accustomed to*.

Example:
What time are you accustomed to getting up?
I'm accustomed to getting up at 6:30 in the morning.

1. What time are you accustomed to/used to ...
   a. getting up?
   b. going to bed?
   c. eating lunch?
   d. eating dinner?
2. What language are you accustomed to speaking at home?
3. What are you accustomed to drinking in the morning with breakfast?
4. What are you used to eating for breakfast?

9j   *Be Supposed* + Infinitive

Form / Function

Son, you**'re supposed to tell** us
where you are going!

Subject	Be (Not) Supposed°	Infinitive	
He	**was supposed**	**to write**	to me.
You	**are supposed**	**to help**	your mother at home.
We	**aren't supposed**	**to go**	into that room.

We use *be supposed* + infinitive to talk about something that is expected of someone or something.

> Kevin **is supposed to rain** tomorrow. (That is what the weather bureau predicted.)
> Kevin **is supposed to be** home by ten. (His parents have told him to do this.)

It **is supposed to rain** tomorrow. (That is what the weather bureau predicted.)
Kevin **is supposed to be** home by ten. (His parents have told him to do this.)

Kevin is supposed to be home by 10:00 every evening. Which of the following things is he supposed to do or not supposed to do?

1. be on time for meals *He is supposed to be on time for meals.*

2. wear dirty shoes inside the house *He is not supposed to wear dirty shoes inside the house.*

3. play loud music until three in the morning _____

_____

4. stay out all night on weekends _____

_____

5. tell his parents where he is going _____

_____

6. tell his parents if he is going to get home later than usual _____

_____

7. talk back to his parents _____

_____

8. leave plates of food and glasses of soda in his room _____

_____

9. use his father's computer without permission_____

_____

10. help his mother lift things when he is at home _____

_____

27 Your Turn

Imagine you have a daughter who is fifteen years old. She doesn't like school, doesn't do her homework, and barely passes her exams. She is only interested in clothes, make up, and going out with her friends. She always asks you for more and more spending money every week. She doesn't work. Make sentences about what you think she is supposed to do and you, her parents, are supposed to do.

Example:
She is supposed to do her homework.

WRITING: Describe Personal Qualities

Write a paragraph about your personal qualities.

Step 1. Choose one of these topics:

1. You want a pen pal in another country.
2. You want to find a future husband/wife.
3. You want to find a roommate to share your apartment.

Step 2. Answer these questions about yourself. Write down your answers. You can add other questions if you wish. Use gerunds and infinitives in some of your answers.

1. What do you like/don't like doing?
2. What do you hate/love?
3. What are you interested in?
4. What do you enjoy doing?
5. What are you good at doing?
6. What are you used to doing?
7. What do you need to do for the future?

Step 3. Write your information in the form of a paragraph. For more writing guidelines, see pages 216–220.

Step 4. Evaluate your paragraph.

Checklist

_____ Did you indent your paragraph?

_____ Did you give information about yourself?

_____ Did you give information that would help you reach your goal (finding a pen pal, a husband or wife, or a roommate)?

Step 5. Edit your paragraph. Work with a partner or your teacher to check your spelling, punctuation, vocabulary, and grammar.

Step 6. Write your final copy.

SELF-TEST

1. It is important _____ on time.

   A. to be   Ⓐ Ⓑ Ⓒ Ⓓ
   B. being
   C. to being
   D. be

2. I went to the bank _____ some
   traveler's checks.

   A. for to get   Ⓐ Ⓑ Ⓒ Ⓓ
   B. for getting
   C. getting
   D. to get

3. She was happy _____.

   A. see me   Ⓐ Ⓑ Ⓒ Ⓓ
   B. me seeing
   C. to see me
   D. to seeing me

4. This coffee is _____ for me.

   A. to sweet   Ⓐ Ⓑ Ⓒ Ⓓ
   B. too sweet
   C. enough sweet
   D. two sweet

5. It wasn't _____ to the beach.

   A. too warm go   Ⓐ Ⓑ Ⓒ Ⓓ
   B. enough warm to go
   C. warm enough to go
   D. too warm to going

6. He loves _____ on the pond in the
   winter.

   A. skate   Ⓐ Ⓑ Ⓒ Ⓓ
   B. go skating
   C. to go skating
   D. going skate

7. _____ an easy form of exercise for
   most people.

   A. Run is   Ⓐ Ⓑ Ⓒ Ⓓ
   B. To run
   C. Running is
   D. Running

8. He left without _____ goodbye.

   A. to say   Ⓐ Ⓑ Ⓒ Ⓓ
   B. saying
   C. say
   D. to saying

9. Thank you _____ me with my
   homework.

   A. to help   Ⓐ Ⓑ Ⓒ Ⓓ
   B. helping
   C. for helping
   D. for to help

10. We aren't _____ this cold weather.

    A. accustomed to   Ⓐ Ⓑ Ⓒ Ⓓ
    B. accustom
    C. accustom to
    D. accustomed

B Find the underlined word or phrase, A, B, C, or D, that is incorrect. Mark your answer by darkening the oval with the same letter.

1. <u>Watch</u> sports on television <u>is</u> <u>a lot of</u> <u>fun</u>.
   A   B   C   D

   Ⓐ Ⓑ Ⓒ Ⓓ

2. <u>It is</u> dangerous for anybody <u>to going</u>
   A   B
   <u>jogging</u> in this park <u>at night</u>.
   C   D

   Ⓐ Ⓑ Ⓒ Ⓓ

3. Some people <u>are</u> <u>good at</u> and <u>have</u> a
   A   B   C
   talent for <u>learn</u> languages.
   D

   Ⓐ Ⓑ Ⓒ Ⓓ

4. We <u>were</u> considering <u>to go</u> on vacation in
   A   B
   June, but we <u>postponed</u> <u>it</u> for another
   C   D
   month.

   Ⓐ Ⓑ Ⓒ Ⓓ

5. Some students <u>go</u> to the library
   A
   <u>to studying</u> because <u>it</u> is <u>quiet</u>.
   B   C   D

   Ⓐ Ⓑ Ⓒ Ⓓ

6. The summers <u>are</u> usually <u>warm</u> in this part
   A   B
   of the country, but this year <u>it is</u> supposed
   C
   to <u>being</u> cool.
   D

   Ⓐ Ⓑ Ⓒ Ⓓ

7. I <u>wasn't</u> <u>accustomed</u> to <u>eat</u> with
   A   B   C
   chopsticks until I <u>went</u> to Japan.
   D

   Ⓐ Ⓑ Ⓒ Ⓓ

8. Many students <u>use</u> the Internet <u>for</u>
   A   B
   do <u>their</u> <u>research</u>.
   C   D

   Ⓐ Ⓑ Ⓒ Ⓓ

9. In some countries, <u>it is necessary</u> <u>to pass</u>
   A   B
   an entrance exam before <u>enter</u> <u>a</u> university.
   C   D

   Ⓐ Ⓑ Ⓒ Ⓓ

10. <u>Traveling</u> to new <u>countries</u> <u>are</u> interesting
    A   B   C
    <u>for</u> most people.
    D

    Ⓐ Ⓑ Ⓒ Ⓓ

UNIT 10

COMPARATIVE AND SUPERLATIVE FORMS

10a Adjectives and Adverbs

Basketball players are **tall.**
They throw the ball **quickly**
and **accurately** into the net.

1. We can make adverbs by adding –*ly* to many adjectives. Sometimes the spelling of the adjective changes before –*ly* is added.

Spelling Rule	Adjective	Adverb
To form most adverbs, add –*ly* to the adjective.	quick	quick**ly**
	accurate	accurate**ly**
	dangerous	dangerous**ly**
	safe	safe**ly**
If the adjective ends in *l*, add –*ly*.	wonderful	wonderful**ly**
	careful	careful**ly**
If the adjective ends in *le*, drop the *e* and add –*y*.	gentle	gent**ly**
	subtle	subt**ly**
If the adjective ends in a consonant + *y*, drop the *y* and add –*ily*.	easy	eas**ily**
	noisy	nois**ily**

2. Some adverbs are irregular. Some have the same form as the adjective or a completely different form.

Adjective	Adverb
good	well
fast	fast
hard	hard
early	early
late	late

3. Adjectives can go before nouns.

He is a **tall** man.

Adjectives can also go after verbs such as *appear, be, become, feel, get, look,* and *seem.*

He is **tall.**
He looks **good.**

4. Most adverbs go after verbs and objects, but adverbs of frequency usually go before all verbs except *be.* An adverb of frequency tells how often something happens. (See page 6 for more information on adverbs of frequency.)

Subject	Adverb of Frequency	Verb	Object
He	**always**	eats	breakfast.

Subject	Verb	Object	Other Adverb
She	drives	the car	**dangerously.**
He	speaks		**softly.**

5. Adverbs can also go before adjectives, other adverbs, and past participles.

He was **surprisingly** polite.

Function

1. Adjectives describe nouns. They have the same form in the singular and plural.

He is a **tall** player. They are **tall** men. (The adjective *tall* describes the nouns *player* and *men.*)

2. Adverbs describe verbs, adjectives, or other adverbs.

He plays **well.** (*Well* describes the verb *plays.*)
He is **incredibly** fast. (*Incredibly* describes the adjective *fast.*)
He plays **amazingly** well. (*Amazingly* describes the adverb *well.*)

[1] Practice

Underline the correct word.

1. It was Mary's birthday, but she was (miserable / miserably).

2. She was waiting (impatient / impatiently) to get a phone call.

3. No one called to wish her a (happy / happily) birthday.

Comparative and Superlative Forms

4. (Sudden / Suddenly), she heard the mailman.

5. She ran to the door (quick / quickly).

6. There was an envelope. She opened it (anxious / anxiously).

7. She was (disappointed / disappointedly). It was an advertisement.

8. Mary felt (sad / sadly).

9. Then her friend called (unexpected / unexpectedly).

10. Mary's friend told her to come to her house (immediate / immediately).

11. Mary put on her (new / newly) dress and left.

12. She arrived at her friend's house and knocked on the door (soft / softly).

13. Her friend opened the door (slow / slowly).

14. All her family and friends were there. They all sang "Happy Birthday" (loud / loudly).

---

2 | Your Turn

Write how you think you do the actions in the list.

Example:
speak
I think that I speak quickly, but I walk slowly.

1. speak
2. dress
3. walk
4. study
5. sing

10b Participles as Adjectives

Form

She's **irritated.**

1. We can often use present participles and past participles of verbs as adjectives.

2. We form present participles with the base verb + *–ing*. We form regular past participles with the base verb + *–ed*. See the spelling rules for *–ing* and *–ed* forms on page 215.

Base Form	Present Participle	Past Participle
amuse	amus**ing**	amus**ed**
annoy	annoy**ing**	annoy**ed**
bore	bor**ing**	bor**ed**
excite	excit**ing**	excit**ed**
frighten	frighten**ing**	frighten**ed**
interest	interest**ing**	interest**ed**
irritate	irritat**ing**	irritat**ed**
relax	relax**ing**	relax**ed**
surprise	surpris**ing**	surpris**ed**

Function

1. Past participles used as adjectives describe someone's feelings.

   She felt **relaxed.**
   The boys were **excited** during the game.

   To show what caused the feeling, we can use a prepositional phrase. Most past participles take the preposition *by*. Others take other prepositions. For example, *interested* takes *in*.

   We were amused **by the children's behavior.**
   He was frightened **by the loud noise.**
   They are interested **in astronomy.**

2. Present participles used as adjectives describe the person or thing that produces the feeling.

   She was having a **relaxing** vacation.
   The boys were watching an **exciting** football game.

3 Practice

Underline the correct word.

1. This was a very (<u>fascinating</u> / fascinated) book.
2. At first I thought it was (boring / bored), but it wasn't.
3. The story was very (exciting / excited).
4. I was very (interested / interesting) in the people in this book.
5. I was (surprised / surprising) by the ending of the story.
6. I was (shocked / shocking) to know it was based on a true story.
7. It is (frightening / frightened) to know that these things can really happen.
8. I read the book quickly because it was so (interested / interesting).
9. I am (interesting / interested) in reading another book by the same author.
10. I don't think I will be (disappointed / disappointing).

4 Practice

Alan and Brenda have been on vacation. Read the dialogue and underline the correct participle in parentheses.

Alan: I was (<u>surprised</u> / surprising) at how good the weather was.
         1

Brenda: Yes, it was really sunny. It was (surprising / surprised).
         2

Alan: It was good to lie in the sun. It was so (relaxed / relaxing).
         3

Brenda: There was a lot to see, too. The museum was (interested / interesting).
         4

Alan: Yes, I was (interesting / interested) in many things there.
         5

Brenda: I was (fascinating / fascinated) by the king's furniture.
         6

Alan: Yes, the furniture was (fascinating / fascinated).
         7

Brenda: But I was (tiring / tired) after the museum.
         8

Alan: Yes, it was (tired / tiring).
         9

Brenda: Now I am (exhausted / exhausting).
         10

Alan: Vacations are always (exhausted / exhausting).
         11

Your Turn

Write one sentence with each of the words in the list.

bored   interested   surprised
boring   interesting   surprising

1. *I think that history is interesting.*
2. _____
3. _____
4. _____
5. _____
6. _____

10c Adjectives After Verbs

Form / Function

The coffee **smells good.**

1. We can use adjectives after verbs of existence, such as *be, get*, become,* and *seem*.

   He **seems nice.**
   Be quiet!
   I'm **getting hungry.**

2. We can also use adjectives after verbs of the senses like *look, feel, sound, taste,* and *smell*.

   You **look tired.**
   The coffee **smells good.**
   This soup **tastes strange.**

*In this use, *get* usually means *become*.

6 Practice

Guests are coming to Ann's house this evening, but things have gone wrong. Complete the sentences with one of the words from the list.

burned   happy   short   tired
dirty   miserable   sweet   wet

1. Ann isn't happy today. She feels ___miserable.___

2. She was cooking and cleaning for hours and hours. She got _____

3. She forgot about the cake in the oven. The cake got _____

4. She went out and it started to rain. She had no umbrella. She got

   _____

5. The dog came in with muddy feet. The floor got _____

6. She put sugar instead of salt in the soup. The soup tasted _____

7. She tried on her new dress but it seemed _____

8. Luckily, when her guests came, they had a good time. She felt _____

7 Practice

Underline the correct word.

1. Tony was getting (<u>hungry</u> / hungrily).

2. The dinner was (ready / readily).

3. The soup smelled (good / well).

4. It tasted (good / well).

5. Tony finished the soup (quick / quickly).

6. His grandmother had cooked (good / well).

7. She cooked some (specially / special) pasta for him.

8. It looked (delicious / deliciously).

9. He looked at the dish (hungry / hungrily).

10. He ate it (quickly / quick) because it was so good.

11. Tony was (happy / happily).

10d *As* + Adjective + *As*; *As* + Adverb + *As*

May and June are twins.
May is **as tall as** June.

1. We can use *as...as* with adjectives and adverbs.

ADJECTIVES					
Subject	Verb (+ *Not*)	*As*	Adjective	*As*	
May	is isn't	as	tall old good funny	as	June.

ADVERBS					
Subject	Verb (+ Not)	As	Adverb	As	
May	learns doesn't learn	as	quickly	as	June.
	runs doesn't run		fast		
	studies doesn't study		hard		
	laughs doesn't laugh		loudly		

2. We can add an auxiliary verb or repeat the first verb at the end of the sentence.

> May is as funny as June.
> May is as funny as June **is.**
> May plays as beautifully as June.
> May plays as beautifully as June **does.**
> May plays as beautifully as June **plays.**

Function

1. We use *as ... as* to show that two people or two things are the same or equal.

> May is **as old as** June. (May and June are the same age.)

2. We use *not as ... as* for the negative form.

> May is **not as funny as** June.

3. When we use *not as ... as* instead of the comparative, it sometimes sounds more polite.

> Ben is **shorter than** Jim.
> Ben is **not as tall as** Jim.

9 Practice

Use the prompts to write sentences with *as ... as* or *not as ... as*.

1. autumn/cold/winter

   Autumn is not as cold as winter.

2. the month of September/long/the month of June

   _____

3. in the United States, September/hot/July

_____

4. in the winter months, California/cold/New York

_____

5. days in winter/long/days in summer

_____

6. September/popular/July for vacations in North America

_____

7. in autumn, plants/grow/fast/in spring

_____

8. in summer, people/dress/heavily/in winter

_____

9. in autumn, flowers/are/colorful/in spring

_____

10. in summer, it/rain/frequently/in spring

_____

10 Practice

Many languages have sayings that include a phrase similar to _as ... as_. Complete the following sayings with words from the list. Then explain how they are different in another language that you know.

a bird	a feather	clockwork	ink	sugar
a dog	a mouse	gold	snow	the sky

1. Mary made a cake. The cake was as light as ____ _a feather._ ____

2. This melon is sweet. It is as sweet as _____

3. Nobody noticed that Tina had come home. She was as quiet as _____

4. We left the children with my sister for the weekend. The children were happy and were as good as _____

5. The coffee she made was very strong, and it was as black as _____

6. She had beautiful blue eyes. They were as blue as _____

7. He left home and moved to the city. Then he felt as free as _____

8. The fish I ate for dinner was bad, and I was as sick as _____

9. George comes to the office at exactly the same time every day. He is as regular as

_____

10. Harry was not old, but his hair was as white as _____

Compare yourself today with the way you were five years ago.
Use *as ... as* or *not as ... as.*

Example:
study hard
Today, I study as hard as I did five years ago.
OR Today, I don't study as hard as I did five years ago.

1. study hard
2. be happy
3. be healthy
4. be poor
5. sleep late

10e Comparative Forms of Adjectives and Adverbs

Form

Fifty years ago, office machines were **slower than** today.

1. Adjectives and adverbs form their comparatives in the same ways.

SHORT ADJECTIVES AND ADVERBS					
Adjective + *-er* + *Than*			Adverb + *-er* + *Than*		
A typewriter is	slow**er than**	a computer.	She can type	fast**er than**	I can.

LONG ADJECTIVES AND ADVERBS					
More/Less + Adjective + *Than*			*More/Less* + Adverb + *Than*		
A computer is	**more** useful **than**	a typewriter.	She types	**less** accurately **than**	I do.

2. We use these rules for spelling the comparative forms of short (one syllable) adjectives and adverbs and for two-syllable adjectives ending in –y.

Spelling Rule	Adjective	Comparative Adjective	Adverb	Comparative Adverb
Add –er to most one-syllable adjectives and adverbs.	cheap	cheap**er than**	fast	fast**er than**
If a one-syllable adjective or adverb ends in e, or a two-syllable adjective ends in le, add –r.	wide	wider **than**	late	later **than**
	simple	simpler **than**		
If a one-syllable adjective ends in a single vowel plus a consonant, double the consonant and add –er.	hot	hot**ter than**		
If a two-syllable adjective ends in a consonant plus y, change the y to i and add –er.	noisy	nois**ier than**		

3. Some adjectives and adverbs have irregular comparative forms.

Adjective	Adverb	Comparative Form for Both
good	well	**better than**
bad	badly	**worse than**
far	far	**farther/further than**

4. We use these rules for using the –er form or the more form of the comparative.

Rules for Using -er or More	Adjectives	Adverbs
Use –er with one-syllable adjectives and adverbs.	small**er than**	fast**er than**
Use –er with two-syllable adjectives that end in a consonant + y.	pretti**er than**	
Use more + adjective/adverb + than with most adjectives and adverbs of two syllables or more.	**more** popular **than**	**more** seriously **than**
Some two-syllable adjectives use –er or more.	angri**er**/**more** angry **than**	
	simpl**er**/**more** simple **than**	
	clever**er**/**more** clever **than**	
	friendli**er**/**more** friendly **than**	
	gentl**er**/**more** gentle **than**	
	narrow**er**/**more** narrow **than**	
	quiet**er**/**more** quiet **than**	
	polit**er**/**more** polite **than**	
	common**er**/**more** common **than**	
	pleasant**er**/**more** pleasant **than**	

Comparative and Superlative Forms

5. We can use a noun after *than*. We can also use a subject pronoun or a possessive noun or pronoun + a verb after *than*. We can omit the verb.

I am taller than **my mother (is).**	I am taller than **she (is).**
My hair is darker than **my mother's (is).**	My hair is darker than **hers (is).**
I study harder than she **(does).**	I study harder than she **(studies).**

6. We can use *less* before an adjective or adverb with two or more syllables.

He is **less serious** than she is.
She speaks **less fluently** than he does.

We do not usually use *less* with one syllable adjectives or adverbs. Instead, we use *not as* (adjective/adverb) *as*.

CORRECT: This CD is**n't as good as** the other one.
INCORRECT: This CD is ~~less good than~~ the other one.

CORRECT: She is**n't** singing **as well as** she usually does.
INCORRECT: She is singing ~~less well than~~ she usually does.

Function

1. We use comparative forms of adjectives and adverbs to show the difference between two things.

Watching television is **more relaxing than** ironing.

2. We use **less** to show a lower degree.

This test was **less difficult than** the last test.

3. If we use a pronoun after *than*, and if we omit the verb, we can use either a subject pronoun or an object pronoun. In formal English, we use a subject pronoun, but in informal English, we use an object pronoun.

FORMAL: She is taller than **I.**
INFORMAL: She is taller than **me.**

If we include the verb, we must use a subject pronoun.

She is taller than **I am.**

4. We use *very* to describe adjectives and adverbs; however, we use *much* with comparative forms of adjectives and adverbs.

It's **very** cold today.
It's **much** colder today than yesterday.

12 Practice

Complete the sentences with the comparative form of the words in parentheses.

1. A bicycle is (quiet) _____ *quieter than* _____ a car.
2. A bicycle is (cheap) _____ a car.
3. A bicycle is (easy to park) _____ a car.
4. A car goes (fast) _____ a bicycle.
5. A car is (expensive) _____ a bicycle.
6. A car is (comfortable) _____ a bicycle.
7. In China, a bicycle is (popular) _____ a car.
8. A bicycle runs (economically) _____ a car.
9. A bicycle is (light) _____ a car.
10. A car is (difficult to use) _____ a bicycle.

13 Practice

Complete the sentences with the comparative form of the words in parentheses.

A.

Ted: You look like your mother.

Nancy: People say that. But, she's really (tall) _____ *taller* _____
        1

_____ *than* _____ _____ *I* _____. My hair
        2   3

is (light) _____ *lighter* _____ _____ *than* _____
                    4   5

_____ *hers* _____.
        6

Ted: Are her eyes (dark) _____
                                    7

_____ _____?
        8   9

Nancy: No. Her eyes are a little (light) _____
                                              10

_____ _____.
        11   12

B.

Jane: I want to fly to Los Angeles tomorrow morning. Are there any flights

        that are (early) _____ *earlier* _____ _____ *than* _____
                            1   2

        the one at 10:00 in the morning?

Travel Agent: Yes, there is. Flight 1620 is at 5:30. And flight 1535 is

(late) _____ 3 _____ 4 flight 1620.

It leaves at 7:00.

Jane: Are there a lot of people on the 5:30 flight?

Travel Agent: No. The 7:00 flight is usually much (crowded) _____ 5

_____ 6 _____ 7 the 5:30 flight.

Jane: I think the 5:30 flight will work (well) _____ 8

_____ 9 the 7:00 flight. Will it be (cheap)

_____ 10 _____ 11 the later flight?

Travel Agent: No, in fact it's $10 (expensive) _____ 12

_____ 13 _____ 14 the other flights.

C.

Ann: Do we have to walk (far) _____ 1

_____ 2 this?

Ken: Just a little (long) _____ 3 . Let's take a rest. Are you

feeling (good) _____ 4 _____ 5

before?

Ann: I feel (exhausted) _____ 6 _____ 7

_____ 8 before.

D.

Jim: The computers in the library are (old) _____ 1

_____ 2 the one I have at home!

Linda: They need to get (modern) _____ 3

_____ 4 computers, but they are very expensive, aren't they?

Jim: Not really. Today, many electronic things are (cheap) _____ 5

_____ 6 they were a few years ago.

14 Practice

Compare each pair of nouns. Use the adjectives. Write your opinion.

1. cats/dogs—friendly

   Dogs are friendlier than cats. OR Cats are friendlier than dogs.

2. fish/lizards—beautiful

   _____

3. spiders/snakes—dangerous

   _____

4. little boys/little girls—noisy

   _____

5. Los Angeles/Chicago—interesting

   _____

6. summers in New York/summers in London—hot

   _____

15 Practice

Complete the sentences using a comparative form of an adverb and your own additional information. You can use the adverbs from the list or your own.

cautiously   dangerously   high
comfortably   fast   slowly

1. The bullet trains in Japan go *faster than the trains in the United States.*
2. The space shuttle flies _____
3. City buses go _____
4. Passengers in a large car usually travel _____
5. In fast traffic, you should drive _____
6. 100 years ago, people traveled _____

16 Practice

Complete the sentences with *much* or *very*.

1. Learning another language is _____*very*_____ difficult.
2. Learning another language is _____ more difficult than learning geography.

Comparative and Superlative Forms

3. English books are _____ expensive these days.

4. Dictionaries are _____ more expensive than books.

5. Chinese is _____ hard.

6. Chinese is _____ harder than English as a language.

7. English spelling rules are _____ unreliable.

8. English grammar rules are _____ more reliable than spelling rules.

---

17 **Your Turn**

Write five sentences comparing people in your family. Use adjectives or adverbs.

Example:
My father is older than my mother.

1. _____

2. _____

3. _____

4. _____

5. _____

10f Superlative Forms of Adjectives and Adverbs

Form

My wedding day was **the happiest** day of my life.

1. Adjectives and adverbs form their superlative forms in the same ways.

SHORT ADJECTIVES AND ADVERBS					
The + Adjective + *-est*			*The* + Adverb + *-est*		
Mt. Everest is	**the** high**est**	mountain.	She runs	**the** fast**est**	of us all.

LONG ADJECTIVES AND ADVERBS			
The Most/Least + Adjective		*The Most/Least* + Adverb	
Which is	**the most** dangerous city?	He works	**the most** happily of us all.

2. We use the definite article **the** before superlative adjectives and adverbs.

> The Crown is **the** best hotel in town.
> It has **the** most expensive restaurant.

3. The spelling rules for short comparative adjectives and adverbs on page 83 also apply to short superlative forms.

Adjective or Adverb	Comparative	Superlative
late	later **than**	**the** lat**est**
hot	hot**ter than**	**the** hot**test**
noisy	nois**ier than**	**the** nois**iest**

4. Some adjectives and adverbs are irregular.

Adjective	Adverb	Comparative Form (Both)	Superlative Form (Both)
good	well	**better**	**best**
bad	badly	**worse**	**worst**
far	far	**farther/further**	**farthest/furthest**

Function

1. We use superlative forms of adjectives and adverbs to compare three or more things.

2. We use *–est* and *most* in superlatives to show the highest degree.

> Antarctica is **the** cold**est** place in the world.
> Tokyo is **the most** crowded city in the world.

3. We use *the least* to show the lowest degree.

> Antarctica is **the least** populated place in the world.

4. We often use the preposition *in* after superlatives. We use *in* with nouns of locations such as *the world,* countries, and cities; and with group nouns such as *the class, my family,* and *the group.*

> Ted is the best student **in the class.**
> The elephant is the biggest land animal **in the world.**
> Sarte is the most expensive restaurant **in New York City.**

Comparative and Superlative Forms

5. We often use the preposition *of* with expressions of time and quantity, and with plural nouns.

> I know three very good restaurants, but this one is the best **of all.**
> Yesterday was the longest day **of the year.**
> He is the youngest **of the students.**

6. We do not use **least** with one-syllable adjectives.

> CORRECT: John is the shortest of my three brothers.
> INCORRECT: John is ~~the least tall of~~ my three brothers.

18 Practice

Complete the sentences with the superlative form of the words in parentheses.

1. Our teacher is Ms. Flint. She gives (clear) _____ *the clearest* _____ explanations of all the teachers.

2. Ms. Flint thinks Linda's handwriting is (neat) _____ handwriting of all the students in the class.

3. We think Peter speaks English (fluently) _____ in our class.

4. All the teachers give us homework, but Ms. Flint gives (difficult) _____ homework.

5. Terry is always the first person to arrive in class. He comes to class (early) _____.

6. Fred is a funny student. He's (humorous) _____ student in the class.

7. Kate takes the class seriously. She's (responsible) _____ student in the class.

8. Tony works (hard) _____ of all the students.

9. He is also (good) _____ student in the class.

10. He gets (high) _____ grades on the tests.

11. He answers the teacher's questions (easy) _____ of us all.

12. Then there is George. He is (bad) _____ student in the class.

19 Practice

Complete the sentences with the correct words.

1. The blue whale is ____*the*____ biggest ____*of*____ all the animals.
2. The giraffe is _____ tallest animal _____ the world.
3. The elephant is _____ biggest _____ all the animals on land.
4. People think the lion is the king and _____ strongest _____ the animals.
5. The ostrich is _____ biggest bird _____ the world.
6. The snail is _____ slowest animal _____ all.
7. Lions sleep for _____ greatest part _____ the day.
8. Antarctica has _____ least number of land animals _____ the world.

20 Your Turn

Imagine there is a fire in your house. You can only take five things away. Which of the five things from the list will you take with you? Think about which is the least expensive, the most expensive, etc. Then discuss your decisions with your partner and the rest of the class. Use comparative forms with the words and phrases in the list or use your own ideas.

Example:
My old photographs are the most important of all, so I will take them.
My radio is the easiest to replace, so I won't take it.

beautiful	cheap	valuable
hard/easy to replace	important	useful

1. your passport
2. your favorite book
3. old photographs
4. your computer
5. an antique vase

6. your sunglasses
7. your jewelry
8. your cell phone
9. your music CDs
10. your radio

10g Comparative and Superlative Forms of Nouns

Of all my favorite foods, ice cream has **the most calories.**

COMPARATIVE NOUNS

1. We use *more* to compare both count and noncount nouns.

   This class has **more students** than that one does.
   Our teacher gives us **more homework** than your teacher does.

2. We use *fewer* with count nouns. We use *less* with noncount nouns.

   This class has **fewer students** than that one does.
   Our teacher gives us **less homework** than your teacher does.

SUPERLATIVE NOUNS

3. We use *the most* with superlative count and noncount nouns.

   This class has **the most students.**
   Our teacher gives us **the most homework.**

4. We use *the fewest* with count nouns. We use *the least* with noncount nouns.

   This class has **the fewest students.**
   That teacher gives **the least homework.**

Function

1. We use the comparative forms of nouns with *more, fewer,* and *less* to compare the different quantities of two nouns.

   I have **more** homework than my friend.
   My friend has **less** homework than I do.
   Your class has **fewer** tests than our class does.

2. We use the superlative forms of nouns with *the most, the fewest,* and *the least* to show the largest and smallest quantity in a group of two or more.

   Tony's class gets **the most** homework.
   Your class has **the fewest** tests.

3. We use *as ... as* to show that things or people are the same in two situations.

   I have 100 CDs. Amy has 100 CDs.
   I have **as many CDs** as Amy (has).

21 Practice

Look at the chart and then complete the sentences.

Food (per 100 gm)	Protein	Carbohydrate	Fat	Calories (kcal)
Bread	7.3	40	2.4	200
Pasta	2.0	14	0.4	60
Pizza	15.0	37	10.0	280
Rice	6.0	52	0.4	225
Ice cream	4.0	21	10.0	190

1. Bread has _____*more*_____ protein than pasta.

2. Pizza has _____ protein.

3. Ice cream has _____ protein than rice.

4. Pizza has _____ fat as ice cream.

5. Rice has _____ carbohydrate than bread.

6. Pasta has _____ fat as rice.

7. Bread has _____ calories than pizza.

8. Pizza has _____ calories.

9. Pasta has _____ calories.

10. Pasta has _____ calories than rice.

22 Practice

Look at the following chart and complete the sentences.

	City A				City B				City C			
People	▓	▓			▓	▓			▓	▓	▓	
Crime	▓				▓						▓	
Pollution	▓				▓	▓			▓	▓		
Doctors	▓	▓			▓	▓	▓					▓
Universities	▓	▓			▓				▓	▓	▓	
Rainfall (a year)	▓				▓				▓			

1. City C has ___the most___ people.

2. City A has _____ people.

3. City A has _____ pollution than City C.

4. City A has _____ doctors than City C.

5. City C has _____ doctors than City A.

6. City B has _____ doctors as City C.

7. City A has _____ universities.

8. City C has _____ universities.

9. City A has _____ universities than City B.

10. City C has _____ rainfall.

11. City A has _____ rainfall.

12. City C has _____ rainfall than City B.

Write five sentences comparing your class with another class, or yourself with someone else that you know. You may use the items from the list to compare.

Example:
grammar
We study more grammar than the other class.

| conversation | grammar | homework | students | tests |

10h The Double Comparative

Form / Function

Buildings are getting **taller and taller.**

1. We use "comparative and comparative" to show that something increases or decreases all the time.

   The weather is getting **colder and colder.**
   Things are getting **more and more expensive.**

2. We can use these sentence structures to show that two things change together or that one thing depends on another thing. The second part of the comparative is often the result of the first part.

The + Comparative Clause	*The* + Comparative Clause
The more you study,	the more you learn.
The sooner we leave,	the sooner we'll get there.

The + Comparative	*The* + Comparative Clause
The harder the test,	the more you learn.
The more people in the room,	the hotter it will get.

24 Practice

Rewrite the sentences about the world today using "comparative *and* comparative" with the underlined adjectives.

1. The world's population is getting <u>big</u>.

   The world's population is getting bigger and bigger.

2. The air is becoming <u>polluted</u>.

   _____

3. Technology is getting <u>sophisticated</u>.

   _____

4. People's lives are getting <u>long</u>.

   _____

5. Computers are getting <u>advanced</u>.

   _____

6. Life is getting <u>complicated</u>.

   _____

7. Buildings are getting <u>tall</u>.

   _____

8. Medicine is getting <u>good</u>.

   _____

9. Forests are becoming <u>small</u>.

   _____

10. The problem of feeding the world's people is getting <u>bad</u>.

   _____

25 Practice

Complete the sentences with "*the* + comparative clause, *the* + comparative clause" or with "*the* + comparative + comparative clause."

1. If the hotel is famous, it is expensive.

   The more famous the hotel, *the more expensive*

   it is.

2. The hotel is near the beach. It is crowded.

   _____ the hotel is to the beach,

   _____ it is.

3. The room is big. The price is high.

_____ the room, _____ the

price is.

4. If you reserve early, the room is good.

_____ you reserve, _____

room you get.

5. The hotel is far from downtown. It is cheaper.

_____ the hotel is from downtown,

_____ it is.

6. You pay more. The service is good.

_____ you pay, _____

service you get.

7. The hotel is near the highway. It is noisy.

_____ the hotel is to the highway,

_____ it is.

---

26 **Your Turn**

A.
Write two sentences about your class or school. Use "comparative and comparative."

Example:
We have more and more tests every year.

1. _____

2. _____

B.
Write two sentences about how you learn. Use "_the_ + comparative, _the_ + comparative clause."

Example:
The better the textbook, the more I learn.

1. _____

2. _____

10i The Same As, Similar To, Different From, Like, and Alike

1. We use *the same* and *the same ... as* to say that things are the same.

   John has a black 2002 Toyota. Jane has a black 2002 Toyota.
   John's car is **the same** color **as** Jane's.
   John's car is **the same** year **as** Jane's car.
   Their cars are **the same.**

2. We use *like* and *alike* to say that things are the same or almost the same. *Like* and *alike* are used in different structures.

Noun	Be + Like	Noun
John's car	**is like**	Jane's car.

Noun	Noun	Verb + Alike
John's car	and Jane's car	**are alike.**
Betty	and Cathy	**look alike.**

   We can also use *alike* with a plural noun or pronoun.

   The twins dress **alike.**
   They talk **alike.**
   They think **alike.**

3. We use *similar* and *similar to* to say that things are different in small ways.

   John has a black Toyota. Paul has a black Mazda. Both cars are small.
   John's car is **similar to** Paul's car.
   John and Paul's cars are **similar.**

4. We use *different* and *different from* to say that things are quite different. We usually use *from* after the adjective *different*. The grammatically correct word is *different from* although some people use *different than* in everyday conversation.

   John has a black Toyota. Mike has a red Volkswagen.
   John's car is **different from** Mike's car.
   John and Mike's cars are **different.**

27 | Practice

Underline the correct form.

1. Mike and Jane live in the town of Homa. Mike lives in

   (the same town / <u>the same town as</u>) Jane.

2. They both live in (the same / the same as) town.

3. Mike and Jane were born in Homa and have lived there all their lives. Mike talks (like / alike) Jane.

4. Mike and Jane talk (like / alike).

5. Ted is Mike's brother. He lives in the town of Chester. Ted lives in a (different / different from) town.

6. Mike and Ted live in (different / different from) towns.

7. Ted looks (like / alike) Mike.

8. Ted and Mike look (like / alike).

9. Mike's truck is (similar / similar to) Ted's truck.

10. Mike's and Ted's trucks are (similar / similar to).

11. Ted is a mechanic. Mike is an engineer. Mike's job is (different / different from) Ted's job.

12. Mike's and Ted's jobs are (different / different from).

28 Your Turn

Work with a partner or a group. Compare the four houses.

Example:
The first house and the third house are alike.

House 1

House 2

House 3

House 4

WRITING: Write a Comparative Paragraph

Write a paragraph that compares your life today with your life five years ago.

Step 1. Think about the following parts of your life today and five years ago. Make notes in the chart.

	Then	Now
1. Schools/classes attended		
2. Homework		
3. Friends		
4. Free time		
5. Interests		
6. Money		
7. Responsibilities		

Step 2. Write sentences about your life then and now. In general, is your life better now than it was? Why or why not?

Step 3. Choose some of your sentences and write them in a paragraph. Give reasons why your life is better or worse now. Write a title to your paragraph, for example, "My Life Then and Now." For more writing guidelines, see pages 216–220.

> My Life Then and Now
>
> Five years ago I attended high school. Now I attend college. The college is farther from my home, and I don't have as many friends there. In college, I have to work harder, and ...

Step 4. Evaluate your paragraph.

Checklist

_____ Did you write a title and put it in the right place?

_____ Did you indent the first paragraph?

_____ Did you say why your life is better or worse now?

Step 5. Edit your work. Work with a partner to edit your paragraph. Correct spelling, punctuation, vocabulary, and grammar.

Step 6. Write your final copy.

SELF-TEST

A   Choose the best answer, A, B, C, or D, to complete the sentence. Mark your answer by darkening the oval with the same letter.

1. Mary is _____ Tina.

   A. as much tall as   Ⓐ Ⓑ Ⓒ Ⓓ
   B. as tall than
   C. as tall as
   D. as taller as

2. As we walked, it got darker and _____.

   A. darker   Ⓐ Ⓑ Ⓒ Ⓓ
   B. more dark
   C. the darker
   D. the darkest

3. This question is _____ than the others.

   A. the less difficult   Ⓐ Ⓑ Ⓒ Ⓓ
   B. less difficult
   C. least difficult
   D. less difficulter

4. This is _____ building in the city.

   A. the most oldest   Ⓐ Ⓑ Ⓒ Ⓓ
   B. the oldest
   C. oldest
   D. most oldest

5. The more you study, _____.

   A. the more you learn   Ⓐ Ⓑ Ⓒ Ⓓ
   B. the more than you learn
   C. you learn more
   D. more you learn

6. It's _____ here in the country than in the city.

   A. more peacefully   Ⓐ Ⓑ Ⓒ Ⓓ
   B. more peaceful
   C. peacefuller
   D. the more peaceful

7. The Bellevue is _____ of the five hotels in this area.

   A. the least expensive   Ⓐ Ⓑ Ⓒ Ⓓ
   B. least expensive
   C. the less expensive.
   D. the least expensivest

8. Ted is a _____ his brother.

   A. better student from   Ⓐ Ⓑ Ⓒ Ⓓ
   B. better student than
   C. gooder student than
   D. best student

9. Carol drives _____ than her sister.

   A. more careful   Ⓐ Ⓑ Ⓒ Ⓓ
   B. more carefully
   C. carefulier
   D. the more carefully

10. The older she gets, the _____ she becomes.

   A. quieter   Ⓐ Ⓑ Ⓒ Ⓓ
   B. more quieter
   C. quiet
   D. quietlier

Comparative and Superlative Forms

B Find the underlined word or phrase, A, B, C, or D, that is incorrect. Mark your answer by darkening the oval with the same letter.

1. This year, computers <u>are</u> <u>more cheap</u> <u>than</u>
                 A   B   C
   <u>last year</u>.
     D

   Ⓐ Ⓑ Ⓒ Ⓓ

2. Our neighbors bought a television set
   that <u>is</u> twice <u>so</u> <u>expensive</u> as <u>ours</u>.
       A   B   C   D

   Ⓐ Ⓑ Ⓒ Ⓓ

3. This is the <u>most funniest</u> movie I <u>have</u>
              A   B
   <u>ever</u> <u>seen</u>.
    C   D

   Ⓐ Ⓑ Ⓒ Ⓓ

4. <u>The more</u> time I spend with my
     A
   grandmother, <u>the</u> more <u>than</u> she
                B   C
   appreciates <u>it</u>.
           D

   Ⓐ Ⓑ Ⓒ Ⓓ

5. It is <u>getting</u> <u>the</u> warmer and <u>warmer</u> as
         A   B   C
   spring <u>approaches</u>.
         D

   Ⓐ Ⓑ Ⓒ Ⓓ

6. My mother and <u>I</u> <u>are</u> <u>like</u> in <u>character</u> and
                  A B C   D
   physical appearance.

   Ⓐ Ⓑ Ⓒ Ⓓ

7. My English teacher <u>is</u> <u>different</u> <u>to</u> my
                    A   B   C
   History teacher <u>in many ways</u>.
                 D

   Ⓐ Ⓑ Ⓒ Ⓓ

8. I am <u>very</u> <u>interesting</u> <u>to see</u> the new
         A   B   C
   exhibit at <u>the Science Museum</u>.
              D

   Ⓐ Ⓑ Ⓒ Ⓓ

9. There are many <u>interested</u> <u>sights</u> <u>to see</u>
                  A   B   C
   <u>in New York City</u>.
         D

   Ⓐ Ⓑ Ⓒ Ⓓ

10. My job and Tony's job <u>are</u> <u>similar</u> each
                       A   B
    <u>other</u> <u>in many ways</u>.
      C   D

    Ⓐ Ⓑ Ⓒ Ⓓ

UNIT 11

THE PASSIVE VOICE

11a Active and Passive Voice Verbs: Simple Present, Simple Past, Present Perfect, Past Perfect, and Future Tenses

The Eiffel Tower **was built** in 1889.
It **was designed** by Gustave Eiffel.
It **is made** of iron, and it **has been repaired** many times.
It **is visited** by millions of tourists every year.

1. A sentence with an active voice verb has a subject, a verb, and an object.

Subject	Active Verb	Object
Gustave Eiffel	**designed**	the Eiffel Tower.

2. A sentence with a passive voice verb has a subject, a verb, and sometimes an agent.

Subject	Passive Verb	Agent
The Eiffel Tower	**was designed**	(by Gustave Eiffel).

3. We form the passive voice with *be* + a past participle. The verb *be* can be in any form: *am/is/are, was/were, has been/have been/had been, be,* and so on. We put the past participle after the form of *be*.

4. For regular verbs, the past participle ends in *–ed.* The past participle of irregular verbs is usually different.

Type of Verb	Base Form	Past Participle
Regular	visit	visited
Irregular	write	written

See page 213 for a list of irregular verbs.

Tense	Active Voice	Passive Voice
Simple Present	Mr. Stone teaches me.	I **am taught** by Mr. Stone.
	Mr. Stone teaches Joe.	Joe **is taught** by Mr. Stone.
	Mr. Stone teaches us.	We **are taught** by Mr. Stone.
Simple Past	Mr. Stone taught me.	I **was taught** by Mr. Stone.
	Mr. Stone taught us.	We **were taught** by Mr. Stone.
Present Perfect	Mr. Stone has taught me.	I **have been taught** by Mr. Stone.
	Mr. Stone has taught him.	He **has been taught** by Mr. Stone.
Past Perfect	Mr. Stone had taught me.	I **had been taught** by Mr. Stone.
	Mr. Stone had taught us.	We **had been taught** by Mr. Stone.
Future	Mr. Stone is going to teach us.	We **are going to be taught** by Mr. Stone.
	Mr. Stone will teach me.	I **will be taught** by Mr. Stone.
	Mr. Stone will teach us.	We **will be taught** by Mr. Stone.
Modals	Mr. Stone can teach us.	We **can be taught** by Mr. Stone.
	Mr. Stone should teach us.	We **should be taught** by Mr. Stone.

5. If we change an active voice sentence to a passive voice sentence, the object of the active voice sentence becomes the subject of the passive voice sentence.

   In a passive sentence, we can express the subject of the active voice sentence as an agent. The agent is stated in a prepositional phrase with *by*.

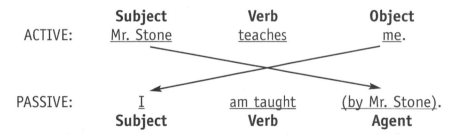

6. We can form the passive voice only with transitive verbs—verbs that have an object.

Subject	Verb	Object
Paolo	wrote	the essay.

The verb *wrote* has an object, so it is transitive, and we can make the sentence passive.

The essay **was written** (by Paolo).

We cannot use the passive form if the verb is intransitive. An intransitive verb does not have an object.

Subject	Intransitive Verb
The book	fell.
The plane	will arrive.

INCORRECT: The book ~~was fallen~~.
INCORRECT: The plane ~~will be arrived~~.

Function

Millions of hamburgers **are eaten** every day in the United States.

We use the passive when we do not know who does an action or if it is not important or necessary to say who does something.

A Van Gogh painting **was stolen** from the National Gallery. (We do not know who stole it.)

1 Practice

Change these sentences from the active voice to the passive voice.

1. Helen invites me.

   I am invited by Helen.

2. Helen invites Ted.

   _____

3. Helen invites us.

   _____

4. Helen invited me.

_____

5. Helen invited us.

_____

6. Helen has invited Jessica.

_____

7. Helen has invited them.

_____

8. Helen had invited me.

_____

9. Helen had invited them.

_____

10. Helen will invite Tony.

_____

11. Helen is going to invite us.

_____

2 | Practice

Change the sentences into passive where possible. When a sentence cannot be changed into passive (because the verb is intransitive), write "No change."

1. I went for an interview last week.

No change.

2. The president of the company conducted the interview.

The interview was conducted by the president of the company.

3. He asked questions in English.

_____

4. I replied in English.

_____

5. I left with a smile on my face.

_____

6. A letter from the company arrived yesterday.

_____

7. My father opened the letter.

_____

8. The president of the company wrote the letter.

_____

9. The job was mine!

_____

3 Practice

What happens when you go to the doctor? Rewrite the sentences in the simple present passive.

1. The nurse weighs you.

You are weighed (by the nurse).

2. The nurse takes your temperature.

_____

3. The doctor takes your blood pressure.

_____

4. The doctor listens to your heart.

_____

5. The doctor examines your chest.

_____

6. The doctor looks at your throat.

_____

7. The doctor checks your lungs.

_____

8. The doctor sends you to the technician.

_____

9. The technician takes blood samples.

_____

10. The doctor then writes a prescription.

_____

4 Practice

Complete the sentences with the simple past passive form of the verbs in parentheses.

1. The world's biggest explosion (cause) _____ _was caused_ _____ by a volcano on the island of Krakatoa in Indonesia in 1883.

2. The explosion (hear) _____ in India and Australia.

3. Half the island (destroy) _____.

4. Only a few people (kill) _____ by the explosion.

5. A very big wave, about 35 meters high, (create) _____ by the explosion.

6. Many small islands (cover) _____ by the wave.

7. More than 160 villages (destroy) _____.

8. Thousands of people (drown) _____ by the wave.

9. Dust from the explosion (carry) _____ to many parts of the world.

10. The weather around the world (affect) _____ for many years.

An erupting volcano

5 | Practice

Jim and Berta saw an old house for sale one year ago, but they did not want to buy it because it needed too much work. They are looking at the house again, and they are noticing some changes. Complete the sentences with the subjects and verbs given. Use the present perfect passive.

1. the outside walls/paint

   The outside walls have been painted. _____

2. the front door/change

   _____

3. the big trees/cut down

   _____

4. a lot of flowers/plant

   _____

5. a new garage/build

   _____

6. the kitchen/modernize

   _____

7. the windows/repair

_____

8. a new bathroom/put in

_____

9. the old gate/replace

_____

6 | Practice

Rewrite the sentences in the passive voice when possible. Use the correct tense. If a sentence cannot be passive, write "No change."

1. German immigrants introduced the hamburger to the United States.

The hamburger was introduced to the United States by
German immigrants.

2. The word *hamburger* comes from the German city of Hamburg.

_____

3. In 1904 at the St. Louis Fair, they served hamburgers on buns.

_____

4. McDonald's® made hamburgers a popular American food.

_____

5. The McDonald brothers opened the first McDonald's® restaurant in California in 1949.

_____

6. The restaurant served only three things: hamburgers, French fries, and milkshakes.

_____

7. People waited outside the restaurant to eat.

_____

8. The business became too big for the McDonald brothers.

_____

9. The brothers sold McDonald's.®

_____

10. Ray Kroc bought the restaurant.

_____

11. Since then, the company has opened over 25,000 McDonald's® restaurants around the world.

_____

12. People eat more than 40 million hamburgers every day.

_____

13. Ray Kroc became a millionaire.

_____

11b The *By* Phrase

The telephone was invented **by Alexander Graham Bell.**

We use a prepositional phrase with *by* in a passive sentence to express the agent when it is important to know who does the action.

The telephone was invented **by Alexander Graham Bell.** (The person who invented it is important to the writer's meaning.)

Hamlet was written **by Shakespeare.** (The person who wrote it is important to the writer's meaning.)

---

7 Practice

Rewrite the sentences in the passive voice. Use the *by* phrase only when necessary. Use the correct tense.

1. Someone built this store in 1920.

This store was built in 1920.

2. An artist painted the ceiling by hand.

_____

3. The famous architect George Emery designed the building.

_____

4. Today, they sell beauty products in the store.

_____

5. They make their creams from plants.

_____

6. They grow the plants in Brazil.

_____

7. They do not test their products on animals.

_____

8. Many famous people use their products.

_____

9. The actress Karen Krone advertises their products on television.

_____

10. They will open another store in New York next month.

_____

8 Practice

Rewrite the sentences in the passive voice. Use the _by_ phrase only when necessary. Use the correct tense.

1. People sell billions of bottles of Coca-Cola® every year.

Billions of bottles of Coca-Cola® are sold every year.

2. People drink Coca-Cola® all over the world.

_____

3. Dr. John Pemberton invented Coca-Cola® in 1886, in Atlanta, Georgia.

_____

4. He sold it as medicine.

_____

5. In the first year, he only sold a few drinks a day.

_____

6. A man named Asa Candler bought the business from Pemberton.

_____

7. He opened the first factory in Texas in 1895.

_____

8. They still make Coca-Cola® there.

_____

9. People do not know the ingredients of Coca-Cola®

_____

10. The company keeps them a secret.

_____

11. World War I made Coca-Cola® popular outside the U.S.

_____

12. They sent Coca-Cola® to soldiers.

_____

13. In 1982, they introduced Diet Coke.®

_____

14. They use many advertisements to make Coca-Cola® popular.

_____

9 Practice

Complete the sentences with the correct form of the verb in parentheses. Use the active and passive voice when necessary. Some verbs are intransitive.

The Olympic Games

The first Olympic games (hold) _____*were held*_____ in the town of
                                              1
Olympia in ancient Greece. They (hold) _____ in 776 B.C. The
                                                    2
games (continue) _____ until about A.D. 394. Then the
                           3
games (ban) _____ by a Roman emperor.
                      4
        A winner of a race in ancient Greece (receive) _____ a
                                                                5
wreath. The wreath (made) _____ of the branches of a special
                                      6
olive tree. Only the winner of a race (recognize) _____.
                                                             7
A runner in second or third place (not, be) _____.
                                                      8
        In 1875, parts of the Olympic stadium (discover) _____
                                                                        9
and people (become) _____ interested in the Olympic games
                             10
again. The French educator Pierre de Coubertin (renew) _____
                                                                   11
the Olympic games in the 1890s. The first modern Olympic games
(hold) _____ in Athens in 1896. After more than
               12
1500 years, Athens (choose) _____ by the organizers
                                       13
to be the place for the first modern Olympics. As in ancient times, the athletes were men.
Women (admit) _____ in 1900. Even in 1932, women
                        14

(not, allow) _____ to participate in more than three events.
15

Since 1896, the Olympic games (hold) _____ every four years.
16

The games (cancel) _____ in 1916, 1940, and 1944
17

because of World Wars. However, in ancient Greece, wars

(stop) _____ for the Olympic games.
18

The Olympic flag (use) _____ for the first time in 1920.
19

The first Olympic village (build) _____ in 1932. Today, before
20

the games, the Olympic torch (light) _____ at Mt. Olympus
21

in Greece. Then it (carry) _____ by runners to the city
22

where the games (hold) _____. Sometimes, the torch
23

(carry) _____ half way around the world. Millions of people
24

around the world (watch) _____ the games. Every four years
25

the games (be) _____ in a different country. Do you know
26

where the next Olympic games (hold) _____?
27

11c The Passive Form of the Present Progressive and Past Progressive Tenses

At the airport, tickets **are being checked.**
Questions **are being asked.**

	Subject	Am/Is/Are	(Not) Being	Past Participle
Present	I	**am**		**asked** questions.
Progressive	He/She/It	**is**	**(not) being**	**understood.**
Passive	We/You/They	**are**		**cheated.**
Past	I/He/She/It	**was**		**asked** questions.
Progressive	We/You/They	**were**	**(not) being**	**understood.**
Passive				

1. The present progressive passive shows that something is taking place right now.

   ACTIVE: Someone **is asking** him questions.
   PASSIVE: He **is being asked** questions.

2. The past progressive passive shows that something was taking place at a specific time in the past.

   ACTIVE: Someone **was asking** him questions.
   PASSIVE: He **was being asked** questions.

3. We can use the *by* phrase if we want to say who or what did the action.

   He was being asked questions **by the airline clerk.**

10 Practice

What is happening at the airport? Complete the sentences with the present progressive passive of the verbs in parentheses.

1. Arriving and departing flights (show) _____ *are being shown* _____ on television screens.

2. Departing flights (announce) _____

3. One flight (cancel) _____

4. Other flights (delay) _____

5. Passports (check) _____

6. Luggage (x-ray) _____

7. People (search) _____

8. Passengers (tell) _____ to wait in lines for their boarding passes.

9. Labels (attach) _____ to luggage.

10. Luggage (take) _____ away on a conveyor belt.

11. Passengers (tell) _____ to wait in the airport lounge.

12. Gate numbers (show) _____ on screens 30 minutes before flight departure.

II Practice

A. At four o'clock yesterday many preparations were being made at the Grand Hotel for the big reception for the president. Complete the sentences with the past progressive passive of the verbs in the list.

bring	decorate	rehearse	tell
cook	make	set	practice

1. A cake _____ *was being made* _____.

2. Food _____.

3. Tables _____.

4. More tables _____ because there
weren't enough.

5. The reception hall _____ with
flowers.

6. Security guards _____ what to do.

7. Music _____ by the band.

8. Speeches _____.

B. What other things do you think were being done? Give five more examples.

1. *Flowers were being arranged.* _____

2. _____

3. _____

4. _____

5. _____

11d The Passive Forms of Modals

Toxic gases **must not be put** into the air.

Dangerous chemicals **must be removed** from the water.

We form the passive of modals with modal + *be* + past participle. We form the passive of modal negatives with modal + *not* + *be* + past participle.

ACTIVE VOICE MODAL			PASSIVE VOICE MODAL	
Subject	Active Modal	Object	Subject	Passive Voice Modal
We	will clean	the air.	The air	will be cleaned.
	can clean			can be cleaned.
	should clean			should be cleaned.
	ought to clean			ought to be cleaned.
	must clean			must be cleaned.
	have to clean			has to be cleaned.
	may clean			may be cleaned.
	might clean			might be cleaned.
	must not pollute			must not be polluted.
	don't have to pollute			doesn't have to be polluted.

12 Practice

A. **People are talking about the environment. Rewrite the sentences in the passive voice.**

1. We must not throw waste from factories into the oceans.

   Waste from factories must not be thrown into the oceans.

2. We should not cut down the forests.

   _____

3. We should protect animals in danger.

_____

4. We must not spray food plants with chemicals.

_____

5. We should recycle bottles and paper.

_____

6. We should save energy.

_____

7. We could use electric cars.

_____

8. We can use other kinds of natural energy.

_____

9. The government ought to ban leaded gasoline.

_____

10. We have to prevent oil spills.

_____

11. We will destroy our planet.

_____

12. We must take action now.

_____

B. Work with a partner. Think of five other things we can do to help our environment.

1. _Paper, metal, and plastic should be recycled._

2. _____

3. _____

4. _____

5. _____

11e *Have* Something *Done*

Bobby **is having his hair cut.**

1. We use *have* + object + past participle to say somebody does a job for us. We do not do it ourselves.

Tense	Subject	Form of *Have*	Object	Past Participle
Simple Present		has		
Present Progressive		is having		
Simple Past		had		
Past Progressive		was having		
Simple Future	He	will have / is going to have	his hair	cut.
Future Progressive		will be having		
Present Perfect		has had		
Present Perfect Progressive		has been having		
Past Perfect		had had		
Past Perfect Progressive		had been having		

2. We can use a *by* phrase to say who performed the action.

   He had his hair cut **by a very good barber.**

13 Practice

This is a busy week for Helen. Write sentences with *have* something *done* and the words in parentheses. Use the correct tense.

1. Yesterday, she (her checks/deposit) to her bank account.

   Yesterday, she had her checks deposited to her bank account.

2. Right now, she (her oil/change).

   _____

3. Yesterday, she (her suit/dry clean).

   _____

4. Tomorrow, she (her teeth/clean).

   _____

5. The day after tomorrow, she (her washing machine/fix).

   _____

6. Yesterday, she (her eyes/test) for new glasses.

   _____

7. Tomorrow, she (her new sofa/deliver).

   _____

8. In two days, she (a tree/cut) down in the back yard.

   _____

9. Yesterday, she (some photos/take) for a passport.

   _____

10. Tomorrow, she (some new business cards/make).

   _____

14 Practice

Karen Krone is a famous movie star. She is very rich and has everything done for her. Read the questions and write Karen Krone's answers. Use a *by* phrase to say who performed the action.

1. Do you style your hair yourself? (Lorenzo)

   No, I have it styled by Lorenzo.

2. Do you drive your car yourself? (my chauffeur)

   _____

3. Will you design your next dress yourself? (Alfani)

   _____

4. Do you cook your food yourself? (my chef)

   _____

5. Do you make your appointments yourself? (my assistant)

   _____

6. Do you clean your house yourself? (my housekeeper)

   _____

7. Did you plant these flowers yourself? (my gardener)

   _____

8. Do you fly your plane yourself? (my pilot)

   _____

9. Do you arrange for your interviews yourself? (my assistant)

   _____

10. Do you buy your groceries yourself? (my housekeeper)

   _____

11f More Phrasal Verbs with Objects: Separable

Form / Function

Remember that phrasal verbs are made of a verb and a particle.

Phrasal Verb	Meaning	Example
call off	cancel something (a meeting, a game, etc.)	They **called** the game **off** because of the storm.
call up	to telephone someone	If you want to go to the movies with Rosa, **call** her **up** and ask her!
pay back	return money to someone	Thanks for the twenty dollars. I'll **pay** you **back** tomorrow.
put back	return something to its original place	Please **put** the books **back** when you're finished with them.
shut off	stop a machine; turn off	How do you **shut off** this machine?
take back	return something (usually to a store)	This CD player doesn't work right. I'm going to **take** it **back.**
try on	put on clothing to see if it is the correct size	Be sure to **try** those shoes **on** before you buy them.
turn up	make the volume louder	I like that song. **Turn up** the radio, please.
turn down	make the volume softer	The television is too loud. **Turn** it **down.**

Replace the underlined words with a phrasal verb + an object. Put the object in the correct place. Remember that sometimes the object can go in two places.

Tom: I can't hear you! Can you <u>make the volume of the television softer</u>?
Sue: Sure.

1. _turn the television down_ _____

Mark: A man <u>telephoned you</u> when you were not here. His name was Thompson.
2. _____
Michele: Did he leave a message?
Mark: Yes, he <u>cancelled the meeting</u> for tomorrow.
3. _____

Janet: I'm going to the department store. I want to <u>return a blouse</u>.
4. _____

Mother: Did you <u>put it on to see if it is the correct size</u> before you bought it?
5. _____

Janet: Yes, I did but I don't like it now. Can I borrow twenty dollars from you? I'll
          <u>give the money to you</u> tomorrow.
6. _____

Mother: OK. But <u>put the milk in its place</u> before you go.
7. _____

Janet: Sure. Anything else?
Mother: Could you please <u>make the television louder</u> before you go so I can hear the
          news?
8. _____

Janet: Do you want me to <u>turn off the oven</u> as well? I think your cake is done.
9. _____

Mother: Yes, please. Thank you.

16 Practice

Answer in complete sentences.

1. What are some things you try on before you buy them?

    I try shoes and pants on.

2. What do you pay back?

    _____

3. What can you turn up and down?

    _____

4. What do you shut off?

    _____

5. Who do you call up often?

    _____

WRITING: Describe a Place

Write a paragraph about a city or town.

Step 1. Work with a partner. Think of a town or city (maybe your hometown or a city you know). Ask and answer questions using the passive voice as much as possible. These prompts may help you.

1. Where is it located?
2. When was it founded?
3. Who/what was it named after?
4. What is/was it famous for?
5. What are some famous places in the city? Who are they visited by? Why?
6. How has your city changed?

Step 2. Write answers to the questions in Step 1.

Step 3. Rewrite your answers in paragraph form. For more writing guidelines, see pages 216–220.

Step 4. Evaluate your paragraph.

Checklist

_____ Did you write a title (the name of the city or town)?
_____ Did you write the title with a capital letter for each word?
_____ Did you indent the first line of your paragraph?
_____ Did you write any sentences in the passive voice?

Step 5. Edit your work. Work with a partner to edit your sentences. Correct spelling, punctuation, vocabulary, and grammar.

Step 6. Write your final copy.

A Choose the best answer, A, B, C, or D, to complete the sentence. Mark your answer by darkening the oval with the same letter.

1. The house _____ recently.

   A. has been painted   Ⓐ Ⓑ Ⓒ Ⓓ
   B. has painted
   C. been painted
   D. was been painted

2. My car radio _____.

   A. was stole   Ⓐ Ⓑ Ⓒ Ⓓ
   B. stolen by someone
   C. was stolen
   D. is stolen by a person

3. _____ in the United States?

   A. People grow rice   Ⓐ Ⓑ Ⓒ Ⓓ
   B. They grow rice
   C. Is rice grown
   D. Is rice grow

4. When _____?

   A. did someone invent   Ⓐ Ⓑ Ⓒ Ⓓ
      paper
   B. was paper invented by someone
   C. someone invented paper
   D. was paper invented

5. Lillian is at the beauty salon. She _____.

   A. is having her hair cut   Ⓐ Ⓑ Ⓒ Ⓓ
   B. is cut her hair
   C. is cutting her hair by someone
   D. has her hair cut

6. Paul's jacket is dirty. He _____ at the dry cleaners.

   A. is cleaning it   Ⓐ Ⓑ Ⓒ Ⓓ
   B. was cleaned it
   C. is having it cleaned
   D. clean it

7. This machine _____ after 6:00 P.M.

   A. must not use   Ⓐ Ⓑ Ⓒ Ⓓ
   B. must not be used
   C. must not be use
   D. not be used

8. I can't hear you. Can you _____ the radio?

   A. turn up   Ⓐ Ⓑ Ⓒ Ⓓ
   B. turn down
   C. turn back
   D. turn it on

9. I always try _____ a pair of pants before I buy them.

   A. it on   Ⓐ Ⓑ Ⓒ Ⓓ
   B. them on
   C. up
   D. on

10. Vicky is at the optician. She is _____ by the doctor.

    A. testing her eyes   Ⓐ Ⓑ Ⓒ Ⓓ
    B. tested her eyes
    C. her eyes tested
    D. having her eyes tested

B Find the underlined word or phrase, A, B, C, or D, that is incorrect. Mark your answer by darkening the oval with the same letter.

1. An island <u>named</u> Easter Island <u>by</u>
             A   B

   the Dutch navigator Jacob Roggeveen in 1772 because he <u>reached</u> <u>it</u>
                                               C D

   on Easter Sunday.

   Ⓐ Ⓑ Ⓒ Ⓓ

2. Many blind people can <u>use</u> <u>their</u> fingertips
                          A   B

   <u>to read</u> what <u>was written</u> on a page.
     C   D

   Ⓐ Ⓑ Ⓒ Ⓓ

3. The nurse Florence Nightingale <u>was call</u>
                                      A

   the Lady of the Lamp <u>because</u> she <u>walked</u>
                      B   C

   from bed to bed in the middle of the night <u>with</u> her lamp.
                           D

   Ⓐ Ⓑ Ⓒ Ⓓ

4. The Royal Flying Doctor Service <u>in</u>
                                  A

   Australia <u>is started</u> <u>by</u> John Flynn <u>in</u> 1928.
         B   C   D

   Ⓐ Ⓑ Ⓒ Ⓓ

5. Workers <u>was gathered</u> from all over Russia
             A

   <u>to build</u> <u>the</u> city <u>of</u> St. Petersburg.
     B   C   D

   Ⓐ Ⓑ Ⓒ Ⓓ

6. When Marco Polo <u>returned</u> from China, he
       A   B

   <u>was written</u> a book about <u>his travels</u>.
     C   D

   Ⓐ Ⓑ Ⓒ Ⓓ

7. The Taj Mahal <u>is consider</u> to be one of the
                  A

   <u>most beautiful</u> <u>buildings</u> <u>in the world</u>.
       B   C   D

   Ⓐ Ⓑ Ⓒ Ⓓ

8. Special diets <u>is needed</u> <u>by people</u> who
             A   B   C

   suffer from <u>certain diseases</u>.
             D

   Ⓐ Ⓑ Ⓒ Ⓓ

9. Moby Dick was <u>a great white</u> whale <u>whose</u>
                  A   B

   story <u>was wrote</u> <u>by the American novelist</u> Herman Melville.
        C   D

   Ⓐ Ⓑ Ⓒ Ⓓ

10. Frozen foods, such as frozen <u>fish</u> and
                           A

    vegetables, <u>introduced</u> in the 1920s when
             B

    people <u>began</u> to buy freezers for
          C

    <u>their homes</u>.
      D

    Ⓐ Ⓑ Ⓒ Ⓓ

UNIT 12

CONJUNCTIONS AND NOUN CLAUSES

12a The Conjunctions *And, But,* and *Or*

Doctors **and** nurses work in hospitals.

Conjunctions are words that join sentences or parts of a sentence.

1. We use the conjunction *and* to join sentences that are alike. *And* can also join one sentence that gives extra information to the other. We use a comma before *and* when it joins sentences.

    I saw the doctor. He gave me some medicine.
    I saw the doctor, **and** he gave me some medicine.

2. We use the conjunction *but* to give opposite or contrasting information. *But* can also join a positive sentence and a negative sentence that talk about the same subject. We use a comma before *but* when it joins sentences.

    A doctor can prescribe medicine. A nurse cannot prescribe medicine.
    A doctor can prescribe medicine, **but** a nurse cannot prescribe medicine.

3. We use the conjunction *or* to join sentences that give a choice. We use a comma before *or* when it joins sentences.

    You can see the doctor at the hospital. You can see her in her private office.
    You can see the doctor at the hospital, **or** you can see her in her private office.

4. When *and, but,* and *or* connect two things (for example, two nouns, two adjectives, two adverbs, etc.) that are not sentences, we do not use a comma.

    You can see a doctor **or** a nurse. (two nouns)
    Nurses must be hard-working **and** patient. (two adjectives)
    The surgeon operated quickly **but** carefully. (two adverbs)

128

5. When we use *and, but,* and *or* to connect three or more items in a series, we use a comma after each item before the conjunction.

   I had a sore throat, a headache, a stomachache, **and** a temperature.

   The doctor told me not to drink tea, coffee, **or** soda.

   The nurse took my temperature, my pulse, **but** not my blood pressure.

6. Do not use a comma when the verb in the second part of the sentence does not have its own subject in that part of the sentence.

   I wanted to see a doctor, but **I saw** a nurse. (Each verb has its own subject. Use a comma.)

   I wanted to see a doctor but **saw** a nurse. (The subject of *saw* in the second part of the sentence is *I*. There is no subject in the second part of the sentence. Do not use a comma.)

1 Practice

Complete the sentences about the body and health with *and, but,* or *or.* Add commas where necessary.

1. We need to eat fruit _____and_____ vegetables for good health.
2. We need vitamins for good health _____ we need only very small amounts.
3. Blood takes food _____ oxygen to the organs of our body.
4. Everyone's blood is one of four basic types: A, B, AB _____ O.
5. O is the most common group _____ there are more people with group A in some countries like Norway.
6. We can live without food for a few days _____ we will die in a few minutes without air.
7. The scalp has about 10,000 hairs _____ about 60 of them fall out every day.
8. The skin is thickest on the palms of our hands _____ the bottoms of our feet.
9. Vitamin A is found in carrots, green vegetables, liver _____ milk.
10. Newborn babies can drink milk _____ they cannot eat vegetables.
11. In the first eight months of its life, a baby cannot sit up, feed itself _____ walk.
12. Our eyelashes _____ eyebrows grow more slowly than the hair on our heads.
13. A newborn baby can see _____ it cannot see things far away.
14. Hair grows faster in the summer _____ when we sleep.

Practice

Add commas where necessary. Some sentences do not need commas.

1. At Mount Rushmore, the heads of Presidents George Washington, Thomas Jefferson, Abraham Lincoln, and Theodore Roosevelt are carved into a mountain.
2. They are the work of Gustave Borglum. He began work in 1927 and died in 1941.
3. Borglum and his workers went up the mountain and they worked even in bad weather.
4. They went on foot or on horseback.
5. Borglum and his helpers went up thousands of times.
6. They used drills and dynamite to remove the rock.
7. The work was difficult and it was also dangerous.
8. In 1941, Borglum died but the work was not complete.
9. His son took over the work and finished it in 1941.

3 Your Turn

What things do you like or not like? Talk about them with a partner.

Example:
I like to eat broccoli, peas, and carrots, but I don't like cabbage.

I like to eat _____, but I don't like _____.

My favorite television shows are _____ and _____,

but I don't like _____.

12b The Conjunction *So*

It started to rain, **so** he opened his umbrella.

So is a conjunction that connects two sentences. *So* gives us the result. We use a comma before *so*.

	Cause	Result
Two Sentences	It started to rain.	He opened his umbrella.
One Sentence	It started to rain,	**so** he opened his umbrella.

4 Practice

Complete the sentences with *but* or *so*.

1. I was tired, _____so_____ I went to bed early.

2. I went to bed early, _____ I couldn't sleep.

3. I couldn't sleep, _____ I got up.

4. I turned on the television, _____ there was nothing good on.

5. I decided to have a glass of milk, _____ I went to the refrigerator.

6. There was no milk in the refrigerator, _____ there was some juice.

7. I drank the juice, _____ it gave me a stomachache.

8. My stomachache got really bad, _____ I took some medicine for it.

9. I was feeling pretty bad, _____ I went to bed.

10. I didn't know what time it was, _____ I looked at the clock. It was 6:00 in the morning.

11. I usually get up at 6:00 to go to work, _____ I got up.

12. I usually feel energetic in the morning, _____ I didn't feel energetic at all!

5 | Practice

Complete the sentences with *and, but, or,* and *so*. Put commas where necessary.

Thomas Edison was a great inventor. He went to school ___*but*___ didn't enjoy it.
                                                                        1

He didn't do his school work _____ the principal of the school told him not to
                                            2

come back. He only went to school for three _____ four months _____ he
                                                      3   **4**

never stopped learning. His mother wanted him to learn _____ she taught him at
                                                                      5

home. She gave him science books. He stayed at home _____ read the books.
                                                                    6

Edison needed money to buy more books _____ he started to work on a train. He
                                                      7

sold candy _____ newspapers. He loved to do experiments. One day he blew up the
              8

office where he worked _____ he lost his job. Edison always worked long hours
                              9

_____ slept for only five _____ six hours a day. Edison invented over
       10   **11**

1,000 items and processes. His most important are sound recording _____ the
                                                                              12

light bulb.

6 | Your Turn

Say three things you need to do. Also say the result. Use *so*.

Example:
I need to do my homework tonight, so I can give it to the teacher tomorrow.

12c *Too, So, Either,* and *Neither*

Linda

Nancy

Linda has curly hair. **So does** Nancy.
Linda has curly hair. Nancy **does too**.
Linda doesn't have straight hair. **Neither does** Nancy.

AFFIRMATIVE STATEMENT	AGREEMENT WITH *TOO*			AGREEMENT WITH *SO*		
	Subject + Verb	*Too*	*So*	Auxiliary Verb	Subject
I like Ken.	I **do,** I **like** him,			do	I.
I am a student.	I **am,*** a student,			am	I.
We are studying.	They **are,*** studying,	**too.**	**So**	are	they.
Bob went to Seoul last year.	Karen **did,** Karen **went** there,			did	Karen.
Tina can drive.	Tom **can,** Tom **can drive,**			can	Tom.

*If no information is repeated from the affirmative statement, we do not contract auxiliary verbs with their subjects when expressing agreement with *too*.

CORRECT:	I am, too.	She is too.	They are, too.
INCORRECT:	I'm, too.	She's, too.	They're, too.

NEGATIVE STATEMENT	AGREEMENT WITH *EITHER*		AGREEMENT WITH *NEITHER*		
	Subject + Verb + *Not*	*Either*	*Neither*	Auxiliary Verb	Subject
I'm not hungry.	I'm **not**, I'm **not** hungry,			am	I.
I don't like football.	Paul **doesn't**, Paul **doesn't like** it,			does	Paul.
I didn't enjoy the movie.	They **didn't**, They **didn't enjoy** it,	**either.**	**Neither**	did	they.
They won't go.	We **won't**, We **won't go**,			will	we.
I can't do that.	I **can't**, I **can't do** it,			can	I.

1. When the main verb is a form of *be* (*am, is, are, was,* or *were*), we use the main verb in the agreement.

   A: I **am** not hungry.   B: Neither **am** I.

2. When the main verb is any other verb in the simple present or simple past tense, we use the auxiliary verbs *do, does,* or *did* in the agreement.

   A: Casey **liked** the movie. B: So **did** I.

3. When the verb is an auxiliary verb + another form of a verb, we use the auxiliary verb in the agreement.

   A: I **am studying**.   B: We **are**, too.

4. When we use *so* or *neither,* we put the auxiliary verb before the subject.

   A: Susan **wasn't** in class. B: Neither **was I**.

5. When we use *too* or *either,* we can also use the entire verb and other information from the original statement.

   A: I **don't like** football.   B: I **don't like it**, either.

Function

1. We use *too* and *so* to agree with or add information to affirmative ideas.

   A: I'm tired.
 B: I'm tired, **too.** OR **So** am I.

   A: Ken is strong.
 B: Ben is, **too.** OR **So** is Ben.

2. We use *either* and *neither* to agree with or add information to negative ideas.

      A: Ken doesn't have a moustache.
      B: Ben does**n't** have a moustache, **either.** OR **Neither** does Ben.

3. In informal conversation, we often use *me too* and *me neither*.

      A: I like Ken.
      B: **Me too.**

      A: I'm not hungry.
      B: **Me neither.**

---

7 Practice

Ken met Monica at a party. They are finding out that they have a lot in common. Write sentences showing agreement using *so* and *neither*.

1. Monica: I love this kind of music.

    Ken: *So do I.*

2. Monica: I haven't been to a party for a long time.

    Ken: _____

3. Monica: I am very shy.

    Ken: _____

4. Monica: I am not good at making conversation.

    Ken: _____

5. Monica: I love to read.

    Ken: _____

6. Monica: I play tennis.

    Ken: _____

7. Monica: I live alone.

    Ken: _____

8. Monica: I came to this city a few years ago.

    Ken: _____

9. Monica: I don't have many friends.

    Ken: _____

10. Monica: I would like to make new friends.

    Ken: _____

8 Practice

Judy and Laura went to a new restaurant. They always agree. Complete the sentences.

1. Judy: I haven't been here before.

   Laura: And I _____*haven't*_____, either.

2. Judy: I like the décor and atmosphere.

   Laura: And I _____, too.

3. Judy: I don't like this dish.

   Laura: And I _____, either.

4. Judy: My food isn't fresh.

   Laura: And neither _____.

5. Judy: My meal is cold.

   Laura: And _____, too.

6. Judy: I can't eat this.

   Laura: And _____, either.

7. Judy: I don't have a napkin.

   Laura: And neither _____.

8. Judy: I didn't ask for a salad.

   Laura: And _____, either.

9. Judy: I am disappointed.

   Laura: And so _____.

10. Judy: I won't come here again.

    Laura: And _____, either.

9 Practice

Fill in the blanks with the names of students in your class and the correct auxiliary.

1. _*Berta*_ wears eyeglasses, and so _____*does Kim.*_____

2. _____ is wearing black shoes, and so _____

3. _____ doesn't have a car, and neither _____

4. _____ always sits in the front row, and so _____

5. _____ wasn't late to class, and neither _____

6. _____ is absent from class today, and so _____

7. _____ answered in class yesterday, and so _____

8. _____ didn't make any mistakes, and neither _____

9. _____ has never been to London, and neither _____

10. _____ wants to learn English, and so _____

10 Your Turn

How do you feel about television, holidays, and music? Make statements. Your partner will agree or disagree. Use *so, neither, too,* and *not ... either.*

Example:

You: I like game shows.

Your partner: So do I, but I don't like police shows.

You: Neither do I.

12d Noun Clauses Beginning with Wh- Words

Form / Function

Mr. Brown, I know **what the answer is.**

INTRODUCTION TO NOUN CLAUSES

1. A noun clause is a dependent clause. It cannot stand on its own. It is connected to a main clause. A noun clause has a subject and a verb.

Main Clause	Noun Clause
I know	what the answer is.

2. There are three kinds of noun clauses.

Type of Clause	Main Clause	Noun Clause
Wh- Clauses (see below)	The students know	what the answer is.
If Clauses (see section 12e)	I don't know	if it's cold outside or not.
That Clauses (see section 12f)	She explained	that she had to leave.

3. We often use a noun clause after expressions like these:

I know	I believe
I don't know	I wonder
Do you know	Can/Could you tell me

NOUN CLAUSES BEGINNING WITH WH- WORDS

MAIN CLAUSE		WH- NOUN CLAUSE		
Subject	Verb	Wh- Word	Subject	Verb
I	don't know	where	she	is.
		when		arrives.
		how		knew.
We	wondered	where	he	was.
		what		was doing.
		why		called.

1. The word order in a wh- noun clause is the same as in a statement: subject + verb.

    CORRECT: I don't know where **he is** going.
    INCORRECT: I don't know where ~~is he~~ going.

2. We use a period at the end of a sentence if the main clause is a statement. We use a question mark at the end of a sentence if the main clause is a question.

    CORRECT: I wonder where she is going. ("I wonder" is a statement.)
    INCORRECT: I wonder where she is going~~?~~

    CORRECT: Can you tell me what time it is? ("Can you tell me" is a question.)
    INCORRECT: Can you tell me what time it is~~.~~

Function

1. We often use wh- noun clauses after verbs such as *know, understand, remember, wonder,* and *believe.* Most of these verbs express thinking, uncertainty, or curiosity.

    Peter left for work this morning. I don't know **when he left.**

2. We use sentences with wh- noun clauses in place of direct questions because they can make a question more indirect, and therefore more polite.

    Direct question: What time is it?
    Wh-clause: Can you tell me what time it is?

11 Practice

A police officer is asking you questions about an accident. You can't remember much and are not sure. Complete the sentences with noun clauses.

1. Police Officer: What color was the car?

   You: I can't remember _what color it was._

2. Police Officer: Who was driving the car?

   You: I am not sure _____

3. Police Officer: How many people were there in the car?

   You: I don't know _____

4. Police Officer: How fast was the car going?

   You: I don't know _____

5. Police Officer: What was the license plate number?

   You: I don't know _____

6. Police Officer: Where were you standing?

   You: I can't remember _____

7. Police Officer: How many other witnesses were there?

   You: I don't know _____

8. Police Officer: When did the accident happen?

   You: I am not certain _____

9. Police Officer: Where was the pedestrian*?

   You: I'm not sure _____

10. Police Officer: How fast was she walking?

    You: I don't know _____

    Police Officer: Thank you. You have been a great help!

    *A *pedestrian* is a person on foot.

12 Practice

A young child is asking his mother a lot of difficult questions. She does not know the answers to them. Complete the sentences with noun clauses.

1. Child: Why is the sky blue?

   Mother: I don't know _why the sky is blue._

2. Child: Who is that girl?

   Mother: I don't know _____

3. Child: What am I going to be when I grow up?

Mother: I don't know _____

4. Child: Where does our water come from?

Mother: I don't know _____

5. Child: Why do stars shine?

Mother: I don't know _____

6. Child: How can a fly walk upside down?

Mother: I don't know _____

7. Child: When do fish sleep?

Mother: I don't know _____

8. Child: How big is the sky?

Mother: I don't know _____

9. Child: What makes the sea blue?

Mother: I don't know _____

10. Child: When am I going to get married?

Mother: I don't know _____

13 Your Turn

Work with a partner to ask and answer polite questions for these situations.

Example:
You: Excuse me. Can you tell me where the restroom is?
Your partner: I'm sorry. I don't know where it is.

1. You are in a department store. You are looking for the restroom.
2. You are in a train station. You are looking for platform 15.
3. You are at the airport. You are looking for the baggage claim area.
4. You are in a supermarket. You are looking for the eggs.

12e Noun Clauses Beginning with *If* or *Whether*

I wonder **if I locked the door.**

MAIN CLAUSE		NOUN CLAUSE WITH *IF* OR *WHETHER*		
Subject	Verb	*If/Whether*	Subject	Verb
I	don't know can't remember	**if** **whether**	I	**locked the door (or not).**

1. *If/whether* clauses have a subject and a verb. There is no comma between the *if/whether* clause and the main clause.

2. When we change a yes/no question to a noun clause, we use *if* or *whether* to introduce the clause. *If/whether* clauses are like yes/no questions, but the word order is like a statement (subject + verb).

    Yes/No Question: **Did** I **lock** the door?
    Noun Clause: I don't know **if** I **locked** the door.

3. The phrase *or not* often comes at the end of the *if/whether* clause.

    I don't know **if** I locked the door **or not.**
    I wonder **whether** the flight has arrived **or not.**

    We can put *or not* immediately after *whether*, but not immediately after *if*.

    CORRECT: I wonder **whether or not** the flight has arrived.
    INCORRECT: I wonder if ~~or not~~ the flight has arrived.

1. *If* and *whether* have the same meaning when they begin noun clauses.

2. As with wh- clauses, we often use *if/whether* clauses after verbs that express mental activity such as thinking, uncertainty, or curiosity.

> I **can't remember** if I locked the door.
> I **don't know** whether he is coming or not.

14 Practice

Brenda was in a hurry this morning. She can't remember certain things she did or didn't do. Rewrite the questions as noun clauses with *if* or *whether*.

1. Did I lock the door? I wonder _if I locked the door._

2. Did I turn off the gas? I'm not sure _____

3. Is the TV still on? I don't know _____

4. Did I mail my bills? I'm not sure _____

5. Did I take my medicine? I can't remember _____

6. Did I feed the cat? I can't remember _____

15 Practice

You have met someone you like, but you are worrying about it. Complete the questions with noun clauses with wh- words or with *if/whether*.

1. What kind of job does he/she have?

   I wonder _what kind of job she has._

2. Does he/she like movies?

   I wonder _____

3. Where does he/she live?

   I wonder _____

4. Is he/she neat and tidy?

   I wonder _____

5. Can he/she play tennis?

   I wonder _____

6. How old is he/she?

   I'd like to know _____

7. Is he/she at home right now?

   I wonder _____

8. Is he/she thinking about me?

I wonder _____

9. Should I call him/her?

I don't know _____

10. Is it too late to call him/her?

I don't know _____

11. Did he/she say he/she would call me?

I can't remember _____

12. Does he/she want me to call?

I wonder _____

16 Practice

You are meeting some people at the airport. Rewrite the questions using noun clauses starting with wh- words or with *if/whether*.

1. Where can I park my car?

   Can you tell me where I can park my car?

2. What time does the flight arrive?

   Do you know _____

3. Is it flight 206 or 208?

   I wonder _____

4. Do the passengers come out here?

   Can you tell me _____

5. Why aren't they here?

   I wonder _____

6. Is the flight delayed?

   I wonder _____

7. Do they know I'll be waiting?

   I wonder _____

8. Will they recognize me?

   I don't know _____

9. How long is the flight?

   Can you tell me _____

10. Did they have a good flight?

   I wonder _____

This is the first day of your new class. Write four statements about things that you are not sure about. Use *if* or *whether* to begin the noun clause.

1. *I wonder if the teacher is nice.*
2. _____
3. _____
4. _____

12f Noun Clauses Beginning with *That*

Form

John realized **that he made a mistake.**
He hopes **that people don't notice.**

MAIN CLAUSE		NOUN CLAUSE WITH *THAT*		
Subject	Verb	*That*	Subject	Verb
John	realized	(that)	he	had made a mistake.
He	hopes		people	will not notice.

A noun clause can begin with *that*. Like other clauses, *that* clauses have a subject and a verb. We can usually omit *that*.

1. We use *that* clauses after certain verbs that express feelings, thoughts, and opinions. Here are some of these verbs.

agree	expect	hope	presume	remember
assume	fear	imagine	pretend	show
believe	feel	know	prove	suppose
decide	figure out	learn	read	suspect
discover	find	notice	realize	teach
doubt	forget	observe	recognize	think
dream	guess	predict	regret	understand

2. We often omit *that,* especially when we speak. The meaning of the sentence does not change.

> Mary: I know (that) she is coming soon.
> John: I hope (that) she does.

3. When the introductory verb is in the present tense, the verb in the noun clause can be in the present, past, or future. It depends on the meaning of the sentence.

> I know she is here.
> I know she will be here.
> I know she was here a few hours ago.

4. To avoid repeating information in giving answers to questions, we can use *so* after verbs like *think, believe, hope, be afraid,* and *guess.*

> Ken: Is Nancy here today?
> Pat: I **think so.** (*So* = "that Nancy is here today")

Negative answers can be formed with *so* or with *not,* depending on the verb.

Question	Affirmative Answer	Negative Answer
Is Nancy here today?	I think **so.**	I don't think **so.** I think **not.***
Did the rain stop?	I believe **so.**	I don't believe **so.**
Are we having dinner soon?	I hope **so.**	I hope **not.**
Is Tony going with us?	I guess **so.**	I guess **not.**
Did you get your grade on the test?	I'm afraid **so.**	I'm afraid **not.**

*"I think not" is formal.

18 Practice

Work with a partner or a group. Write sentences that give your own opinion about each statement. Start your sentences with *I believe/think that* or *I don't believe/think that.*

1. People can live without light.

   I don't believe that people can live without light.

2. It is difficult for some people to learn languages.

   _____

3. There are too many talk shows on television.

   _____

4. Men have shorter lives than women.

   _____

5. People will drive cars with atomic power in our lifetime.

   _____

6. Computers will have emotions.

   _____

7. People will be happy all the time.

   _____

8. We will stop having zoos in fifty years.

   _____

Write two more opinions.

9. _____

10. _____

19 Practice

Complete the sentences with the verbs in parentheses and *so* or *not*.

1. Ken: Do we have class today?

   Sue: (think) *I think so*_____. There is no change that I know of.

2. Ken: Can you lend me your book until tomorrow?

   Sue: (be afraid) _____. I need it tonight.

3. Pat: Is John coming to class today?

   Lillian: (think) _____. I just saw him. He was walking

   this way.

4. Pat: Are we going to have a test today?

Lillian: (believe) _____. The teacher just told me to be ready

for it.

5. Pat: Is it going to be an essay?

Lillian: (guess) _____. The other tests have been essays.

6. Pat: Are you ready for it?

Lillian: (hope) _____. I studied all night.

7. Janet: Do you have an extra pen?

Ben: (think) _____. I always carry an extra one.

8. Janet: Can we use a dictionary during the test?

Ben: (afraid) _____. Our teacher never lets us do that.

20 Your Turn

Work with a partner. Take turns asking and answering the following questions. Add some questions of your own. Answer with the verbs in this section.

Example:

You: Is your English improving?

Your partner: I think so. It's improving very slowly.

                OR No, I don't think so. I still don't understand the present perfect.

1. Is your English improving?

2. Would you like to be a teacher?

3. Would you like to live in a different country from the one you grew up in?

4. Do you think you will change in the future?

Conjunctions and Noun Clauses

12g Expressions that Introduce Noun Clauses with *That*

It is true that a cat is not able to taste sweet things.

1. We can use *that* clauses after expressions with *be* + an adjective, or with *be* + a past participle. These expressions show feeling. We can omit the word *that*.

Main Clause	*That* Clause
I am sorry	(that) you couldn't come.
I am disappointed	(that) I failed the test.

2. Here is a list of some of the adjectives and past participles that can introduce *that* clauses.

be afraid	be delighted	be happy	be proud	be terrified
be amazed	be disappointed	be horrified	be sad	be thrilled
be angry	be fortunate	be impressed	be shocked	be worried
be aware	be furious	be lucky	be sure	it is a fact
be convinced	be glad	be pleased	be surprised	it is true

21 Practice

Look at the following facts and write your opinion about each one. Use a *that* clause and one of the expressions from the list.

I am (not) aware that   I am (not) surprised that
It is (not) a fact that   It is (not) true that

1. There is a town called "Chicken" in Alaska.

   I am surprised that there is a town called Chicken in Alaska.

2. Rice is the chief food for half the people in the world.

   _____

3. There are 15,000 different kinds of rice.

_____

4. Women live longer today than they did 100 years ago.

_____

5. Women live longer than men.

_____

6. Clouds are higher during the day than during the night.

_____

7. Men laugh longer, more loudly, and more often than women.

_____

8. Everyone dreams.

_____

9. The elephant is the largest animal on land.

_____

10. People in India drink tea with a lot of milk, sugar, and spices.

_____

11. Hair grows faster at night.

_____

12. The smallest country in the world is Vatican City.

_____

22 Your Turn

Give your opinion about five things or five people. Use a _that_ clause with one of the following expressions or others from this section.

Example:
I am pleased that I passed the test.

I'm angry   I'm proud
I'm glad   I'm surprised
I'm pleased

WRITING: Describe an Event

Write a personal letter that describes something that happened to you in your life.

Step 1. Write sentences about an event that happened to you recently that made you feel sad, happy, upset, etc. Use conjunctions and noun clauses in your answers.

1. When did it happen?

2. Where did it happen?

3. What happened?

4. What was the result?

5. How did you feel about it?

Step 2. Write a letter to a friend or family member about this experience. Use the sentences from Step 1 and the following model as a guide. For more writing guidelines, see pages 216–220.

> January 3, 20XX
>
> Dear Meg,
>
> Happy New Year! We had a good holiday season here. I feel especially happy because of a great thing that happened to me last week.
>
> You know that I have been seeing Joe for about a year. Well, on Tuesday, he came over to our house and _____
> _____
> _____
> _____
> _____
>
> You can imagine how I felt. Please write back and let me know what you think.
>
> Your friend,
> Cathy

Step 3. Evaluate your letter.

Checklist

_____ Did you put the date at the top of your letter?

_____ Did you start your letter with "Dear" and the person's name?

_____ Did you write an introductory paragraph?

_____ Did you describe the event that happened to you?

_____ Did you write a concluding paragraph?

_____ Did you end your letter with a phrase such as "Yours truly" or "Love" and your name?

Step 4. Edit your work. Work with a partner or your teacher to edit your paragraph. Check spelling, vocabulary, and grammar.

Step 5. Write your final copy.

SELF-TEST

A Choose the best answer, A, B, C, or D, to complete the sentence. Mark your answer by darkening the oval with the same letter.

1. Tom: I hate fish.
   Jack: I _____. I don't like the smell.

   A. too   Ⓐ Ⓑ Ⓒ Ⓓ
   B. either
   C. neither
   D. do, too

2. Ken was born in Hong Kong. So _____ his sister.

   A. didn't   Ⓐ Ⓑ Ⓒ Ⓓ
   B. did
   C. was
   D. wasn't

3. I wonder _____ the movie.

   A. if liked she   Ⓐ Ⓑ Ⓒ Ⓓ
   B. if did she like
   C. if she liked
   D. if or not she liked

4. I don't know _____.

   A. what job she does   Ⓐ Ⓑ Ⓒ Ⓓ
   B. if job she does
   C. what does she job
   D. what job does she

5. It is a fact _____ everybody dreams.

   A. that   Ⓐ Ⓑ Ⓒ Ⓓ
   B. if
   C. what
   D. whether

6. He had a rash, a headache, _____ a temperature from the bad food.

   A. but   Ⓐ Ⓑ Ⓒ Ⓓ
   B. so
   C. and
   D. or

7. I have a computer, _____ I read the news on the Internet.

   A. so   Ⓐ Ⓑ Ⓒ Ⓓ
   B. and
   C. or
   D. but

8. Bill: Are we having a test today?
   Lisa: _____.

   A. I hope not   Ⓐ Ⓑ Ⓒ Ⓓ
   B. I don't hope so
   C. I don't guess so
   D. I don't think

9. Chris: Is the teacher here today?
   Pat: _____.

   A. I think   Ⓐ Ⓑ Ⓒ Ⓓ
   B. I don't hope
   C. I guess so
   D. I believe

10. Ken doesn't have a car and _____.

    A. neither does not   Ⓐ Ⓑ Ⓒ Ⓓ
       John
    B. neither does John
    C. neither John does
    D. John doesn't neither

Conjunctions and Noun Clauses

B Find the underlined word or phrase, A, B, C, or D, that is incorrect. Mark your answer by darkening the oval with the same letter.

1. It is a fact what about two-thirds of your
   A   B

   body is water.
      C D

Ⓐ Ⓑ Ⓒ Ⓓ

2. Chimpanzees are very intelligent creatures
             A   B

   and too are dolphins.
      C   D

Ⓐ Ⓑ Ⓒ Ⓓ

3. I asked that salt water freezes at a
        A   B

   lower temperature than fresh water.
   C   D

Ⓐ Ⓑ Ⓒ Ⓓ

4. Most vegetarians eat dairy products, such
                A

   as cheese and milk, and vegans avoid all
      B   C

   animal products.
      D

Ⓐ Ⓑ Ⓒ Ⓓ

5. Many island people in Indonesia and the
                       A

   Philippines live on boats but in houses
           B   C

   made of wood over the water.
        D

Ⓐ Ⓑ Ⓒ Ⓓ

6. I think if the most popular sport
      A   B   C

   in Japan is baseball.
        D

Ⓐ Ⓑ Ⓒ Ⓓ

7. I don't know if makes the sky blue,
           A   B   C

   do you?
   D

Ⓐ Ⓑ Ⓒ Ⓓ

8. I wonder if or not a person can grow after
         A   B   C   D

   the age of eighteen?

Ⓐ Ⓑ Ⓒ Ⓓ

9. Picasso was a painter who painted in
         A   B

   several different styles, but greatly
                C

   influenced other painters of his time.
          D

Ⓐ Ⓑ Ⓒ Ⓓ

10. Can you tell me how far is it from here to
           A   B   C   D

   the train station?

Ⓐ Ⓑ Ⓒ Ⓓ

UNIT 13

ADJECTIVE AND ADVERB CLAUSES

13a Adjective Clauses with *Who, Whom,* and *That* Referring to People

A pilot is a person **that flies airplanes.**
I know a man **who is a pilot.**

1. An adjective clause is used with a main clause. An adjective clause describes or gives information about a noun in the main clause.

MAIN CLAUSE	ADJECTIVE CLAUSE
A pilot is a person	**that flies airplanes.**
I know a man	**who is a pilot.**

2. *Who* and *that* are relative pronouns. Relative pronouns begin adjective clauses.

3. We use *who* or *that* to refer to people. *Who* and *that* can be the subject of an adjective clause.

MAIN CLAUSE	ADJECTIVE CLAUSE		
	Subject	Verb	
There is the woman	**who**	flew	the plane.
There's the flight attendant	**that**	helped	us.

4. *Whom* also refers to people. In an adjective clause, *whom* is always an object.

MAIN CLAUSE	ADJECTIVE CLAUSE		
	Object	Subject	Verb
That's the pilot	**whom**	I	know.

Whom is very formal English. When writing, we use *whom* only in formal situations such as writing for school. When speaking, we use *whom* only in formal situations such as giving a speech. We use *that* or *who,* not *whom,* as an object relative pronoun in ordinary speech and writing.

5. An adjective clause comes after the noun it describes. Sometimes the main clause comes in two parts.

> The pilot whom I know is young.
> Main Clause: The pilot is young
> Adjective Clause: whom I know
>
> CORRECT: The **pilot whom** I know is young.
> INCORRECT: The pilot is young ~~whom I know.~~

1 Practice

Match the definitions with the correct adjective clause.

__e__ **1.** A pilot is a person   **a.** who rides bikes.

_____ **2.** A jockey is a person   **b.** who sails ships.

_____ **3.** A sailor is a person   **c.** who rides racehorses.

_____ **4.** A race car driver is a person   **d.** who travels into space.

_____ **5.** An astronaut is a person   **e.** who flies planes.

_____ **6.** A cyclist is a person   **f.** who drives fast cars.

2 Practice

Complete the definitions with an adjective clause using *who* or *that*. Use the phrases from the list.

cuts men's hair	serves people in a restaurant
fixes cars	trains athletes
fixes teeth	works in a bank
helps sick people	writes for a newspaper

1. A mechanic _is a person who fixes cars._

2. A barber _____

3. A doctor _____

4. A coach _____

5. A waiter _____

6. A journalist _____

7. A dentist _____

8. A teller _____

Practice

Read the first two sentences. Then complete the third sentence with an adjective clause. Use *who* if the relative pronoun is the subject. Use *whom* if it is the object.

1. That's the woman. I dated her a few times last year.

    That's the woman _whom I dated a few times last year._

2. She's the one. She had a lot of money.

    She's the one _____

3. She had an assistant. The assistant did everything for her.

    She had an assistant _____

4. She had a driver. She paid him to take care of her three cars.

    She had a driver _____

5. She had a cook. He made fantastic food.

    She had a cook _____

6. Unfortunately, she wasn't the woman. I wanted to marry her.

    Unfortunately, she wasn't the woman _____

7. I found another woman. She works as a librarian.

    I found another woman _____

8. She says I'm the man. She wants to marry me.

    She says I'm the man _____

9. She's the woman. She will be my wife.

    She's the woman _____

10. We'll be two people. We won't have much money.

    We'll be two people _____

11. But we'll be two people. We will be happy.

    But we'll be two people _____

4 Practice

Combine the two sentences into one sentence. Use *who* if the relative pronoun is a subject. Use *whom* if it is an object.

1. Grace Kelly was an actress. This actress became Princess Grace of Monaco.

    Grace Kelly was an actress who became Princess Grace
    of Monaco.

2. The Beatles were four young men. These young men became famous all over the world.

    _____

3. Brad Pitt is an actor. This actor stars in a lot of popular movies.

_____

4. The man was a movie director. We saw him in the restaurant.

_____

5. James Dean was an actor. This actor died young.

_____

6. The opera singer isn't Spanish. We heard him last night.

_____

7. Louis Armstrong was a famous jazz musician. This musician played the trumpet.

_____

8. There was a beautiful actress. We met her at the party.

_____

9. The singer is giving a concert here next week. I like her so much.

_____

10. Celine Dion is a singer. I'm sure you have heard her.

_____

11. Who is that detective on TV? He always solves the problem.

_____

12. Sophia Loren is a famous movie star. Everybody knows her.

_____

5 | Your Turn

Make sentences with adjective clauses to describe these people.

Example:
a friend
A friend is someone who tells you the truth.

a friend
a teacher
a leader
a grandfather

13b Adjective Clauses with *That* and *Which* Referring to Things

An orange is a kind of fruit **that** has a lot of vitamin C.

1. We use *who (whom)/that* to refer to people. We use *that/which* to refer to things.

   Casimir Funk was the man **who/that** invented the word "vitamin".
   An orange is a fruit **that/which** has a lot of vitamin C.

2. *That* and *which* can be subject relative pronouns or object relative pronouns.

   You must get the vitamins **that/which** are important to your health.
   (*That/which* is the subject of the verb *are.*)

   The vitamins **that/which** I take are expensive.
   (*That/which* is the object of the verb *take.*)

3. When an adjective clause has a subject relative pronoun, its verb agrees with the word that the relative pronoun refers to.

   A fruit that **is** healthy is the orange.

   A person who **plays** sports needs a lot of energy.

   It is important to eat vegetables that **are** good for you.

   People who **play** sports need a lot of energy.

6 Practice

Complete the sentences with _who_ or _which_. Then check whether you think the sentences are true or false.

1. A person <u>who</u> drinks a lot of water is healthy. T _____ F _____
2. Food _____ is fresh is good for you. T _____ F _____
3. Onions are vegetables _____ make you cry. T _____ F _____
4. Carrots are vegetables _____ make your hair red. T _____ F _____
5. Children _____ eat a lot of butter and sugar grow tall. T _____ F _____
6. People _____ drink a lot of coffee sleep a lot. T _____ F _____
7. Foods _____ have a lot of sugar and fat can make you fat. T _____ F _____
8. People _____ eat a lot of vegetables are healthy. T _____ F _____
9. A person _____ exercises is healthy. T _____ F _____
10. A child _____ eats a lot of candy can develop bad teeth. T _____ F _____
11. Spinach is a food _____ is good for you. T _____ F _____
12. Milk is a food _____ is important for babies. T _____ F _____

7 Practice

Underline the correct verb in parentheses.

1. Australia is a country that (have / <u>has</u>) some special animals.
2. Kangaroos are animals that (live / lives) in Australia.
3. A kangaroo is an animal that (carry / carries) its baby in a pouch.
4. The ostrich is also a bird that (live / lives) in Australia.
5. Ostriches are birds that (run / runs) very fast.
6. An ostrich is a bird that (doesn't / don't) fly.
7. I met some people who (have / has) ostrich farms.
8. Ostriches have feathers that (is / are) beautiful.
9. Some animals that (live / lives) in New Zealand are special too.
10. Kiwis are birds that (live / lives) in New Zealand.
11. A kiwi is a bird that (have / has) very small wings and cannot fly.
12. People who (live / lives) in New Zealand are often called Kiwis.

Adjective and Adverb Clauses

13c Omission of *Who*, *That*, and *Which*

That's the funny tourist we met yesterday.

1. When the relative pronoun *who (whom), which,* or *that* is the object of an adjective clause, we can leave it out.

   He's the funny tourist **that** we met yesterday.
   OR He's the funny tourist we met yesterday. (*That* is left out.)

2. We cannot leave out *who, which,* and *that* when they are the subject of the sentence.

   CORRECT: The man who talked to us yesterday is funny.
   INCORRECT: ~~The man talked to us yesterday is funny.~~ (*Who* cannot be left out.)

---

8 Practice

Complete the sentences with the relative pronouns *who, that,* or *which*. If the relative pronoun can be left out, write *X*.

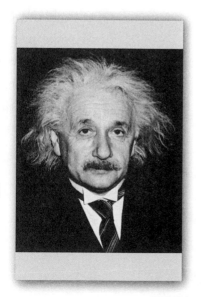

1. Albert Einstein is a name _____*X*_____ everybody knows.

2. Albert Einstein was a genius _____*who*_____ started to speak when he was three years old.

3. Albert was a boy _____ hated school, but he loved to read at home.

4. Science was the subject _____ he loved the most.

5. He had a violin _____ he played often.

6. After his graduation from college in 1900, Einstein was a young man _____ could not find a job.

7. After Einstein graduated from college in 1900, he had a friend _____ helped him get a job.

8. He got a job in a government office _____ he didn't like very much.

9. Einstein was a man _____ wanted to find answers to many difficult questions.

10. Einstein had many ideas _____ changed the world.

11. He was a man _____ people didn't understand.

12. Einstein was a man _____ often forgot things.

13. He wore a coat _____ was old.

14. Clothes were things _____ were not important to him.

15. In 1922, he received a prize _____ made him famous. It was the Nobel Prize.

16. Princeton, New Jersey, was the town in the United States _____ became Einstein's home.

17. When Einstein died at the age of 76 in New Jersey, scientists _____ admired his work were sad.

18. Because of Einstein, scientists have important knowledge _____ they can use to help us understand the universe.

13d Adjective Clauses with *Whose*

A: What's a mermaid?
B: That's a legendary woman **whose** body is like a fish from the waist down.

1. We use the relative pronoun *whose* to show possession. We use *whose* instead of possessive adjectives like *my, your,* and *his* with people, animals, and things.

   > A mermaid is a legendary woman. **Her** body is like a fish from the waist down.
   > A mermaid is a legendary woman **whose** body is like a fish from the waist down.

   > I know the man. **His** house is by the river.
   > I know the man **whose** house is by the river.

2. We use *whose* to refer to people. In informal English, we also use *whose* to refer to things.

   > New York is a city **whose** restaurants are very good.

3. Do not confuse *whose* with *who's*. They sound the same, but their meanings are different.

	Form	Example
Who's	A contraction of *who is*	A: **Who's** that? B: It's Jack.
Whose	A relative pronoun	That's the man **whose** car was stolen.

9 | Practice

Combine the sentences using *whose*.

1. The student will win the prize. The student's essay is the best.

   The student whose essay is the best will win the prize.

2. I know a man. His brother is a guitarist in a pop group.

   _____

3. I won't go out with a man. His hair is always a mess.

   _____

4. I hear someone. Her voice is beautiful.

   _____

5. Those are the girls. Their Portuguese is almost perfect.

   _____

6. I once met someone. His conversations were always about food.

   _____

7. I have a friend. Nobody can pronounce his last name.

_____

8. I like people. Their lives are organized.

_____

10 Practice

Complete the questions with _who_ for people, _that_ for things, and _whose_ to show possession. Then circle the answer that you think is correct.

1. Who was the person ____who____ invented the light bulb?

   a. George Washington   **b.** Thomas Edison   **c.** Vincent Van Gogh

2. What is the name of the long river _____ is in Africa?

   a. The Nile   **b.** The Mississippi   **c.** The Seine

3. What is the name of the painter _____ most famous painting is the _Mona Lisa_?

   a. Pablo Picasso   **b.** Leonardo da Vinci   **c.** Jean Renoir

4. What is the name of the writer _____ wrote _Hamlet_?

   a. Charles Dickens   **b.** William Shakespeare   **c.** Ernest Hemingway

5. What's the name of the country _____ capital city is Buenos Aires?

   a. Mexico   **b.** Spain   **c.** Argentina

6. What is the name of the South American country _____ people speak Portuguese?

   a. Argentina   **b.** Chile   **c.** Brazil

7. What is the name of the woman _____ helped the poor and sick in India?

   a. Mother Teresa   **b.** Florence Nightingale   **c.** Princess Diana

8. What is the name of the country _____ has the most people in the world?

   a. The United States   **b.** Japan   **c.** China

9. What is the name of the man _____ was the first to walk on the moon?

   a. Neil Armstrong   **b.** Frank Sinatra   **c.** John Kennedy

10. What is the name of the man _____ home was Graceland, in Memphis, Tennessee?

    a. John Lennon   **b.** Mick Jagger   **c.** Elvis Presley

13e Adjective Clauses with Prepositional Phrases

A measuring tape is something you measure things **with**.

1. The relative pronouns *who (whom)*, *that*, and *which* can be the objects of prepositions in an adjective clause.

   I was sitting on a chair. It was uncomfortable. The chair **that I was sitting on** was uncomfortable.

2. There are two structures for prepositional phrases with relative pronoun objects. In informal English, we can also use different relative pronouns.

THE RELATIVE PRONOUN REFERS TO A THING

Rules	Main Clause	Adjective Clause	End of Main Clause
Informal English: The preposition goes at the end of the adjective clause.	The chair	**that** I was sitting **on** / **which** I was sitting **on** / I was sitting **on**	was uncomfortable.
Formal English: The preposition goes at the beginning of the adjective clause. The relative pronoun must be *which*.	The chair	**on which** I was sitting	was uncomfortable.

THE RELATIVE PRONOUN REFERS TO A PERSON

Rules	Main Clause	Adjective Clause	End of Main Clause
Informal English: The preposition goes at the end of the adjective clause.	The woman	**that** I was talking **to** / **who** I was talking **to** / I was talking **to**	was interesting.
Formal English: The preposition goes at the beginning of the adjective clause. The relative pronoun must be *whom*.	The woman	**to whom** I was talking	was interesting.

3. The choices of relative pronouns are the same as for other kinds of objects. In informal English, you can omit the relative pronoun because it is an object.

> The woman **that/who** I was talking **to** was interesting.
> OR The woman I was talking **to** was interesting.

But when we use formal English and put the preposition first, we must use the relative pronoun.
> CORRECT: The woman **to whom** I was talking was interesting.
> INCORRECT: The woman ~~to I was talking~~ was interesting.

II Practice

First complete the definitions using informal English. Then write the definitions again using formal English. Use the phrases in the list.

are honest with	get information from	sleep in
care for	laugh at	travel in
climb on	look through	work toward
drink from	play with	write with
eat with	sit on	

1. Informal: A pen is something you _write with._

   Formal: _A pen is something with which you write._

2. Informal: A bed is something you _____

   Formal: _____

3. Informal: A cup is something you _____

   Formal: _____

4. Informal: A goal is something you _____

   Formal: _____

5. Informal: A chair and a stool are things you _____

   Formal: _____

6. Informal: A spoon is something you _____

   Formal: _____

7. Informal: A best friend is a person you _____

   Formal: _____

8. Informal: A ladder is something you _____

   Formal: _____

9. Informal: The Internet is something you _____

   Formal: _____

10. Informal: A circus clown is someone you _____

      Formal: _____

11. Informal: A car is something you _____

      Formal: _____

12. Informal: A ball is a thing you _____

      Formal: _____

13. Informal: A telescope is something you _____

      Formal: _____

14. Informal: A sick person is someone you _____

      Formal: _____

---

12   Your Turn

Choose one of the following objects for the class to guess. The class asks questions about the object. Use informal English, and do not use *which* or *that*.

Example:

Your classmate: Is it something you speak into?
You: Yes, it is. OR No, it isn't.

a can opener	a notebook	an umbrella
a cushion	a telephone	

13f Adverb Clauses with *Because*

Form

Carlos is happy **because he passed the test.**

1. A main clause has a subject and a verb and can stand alone as a complete sentence.

   Carlos is happy.

2. An adverb clause also has a subject and a verb, but it is not a complete sentence. We must use it with a main clause.

MAIN CLAUSE			ADVERB CLAUSE			
Subject	Verb		Conjunction	Subject	Verb	
Carlos	is	happy	because	he	passed	the test.

3. *Because* is a conjunction that can begin an adverb clause.

4. An adverb clause can come at the beginning or at the end of a sentence. It has the same meaning. If the adverb clause comes at the beginning, we put a comma after the adverb clause.

   Carlos is happy **because he passed the test.**
   Because Carlos passed the test, he is happy.

Function

We use the conjunction *because* to give a reason for something or to say why something happens. *Because* answers the question *why*.

   Carlos is happy. **Why** is he happy? He's happy **because he passed the test.**

13 Practice

Combine the sentences with *because* in two different ways as in the example. Use correct punctuation.

1. Pete failed the test. He didn't study.

   Pete failed the test because he didn't study.

   Because Pete didn't study, he failed the test.

2. Pete didn't have time to study. He was working.

   _____

   _____

3. Pete worked. He needed money.

   _____

   _____

4. Pete needed money. He wanted to help his family.

_____

_____

5. Pete's family had problems. His father lost his job.

_____

_____

6. His father lost his job. The company closed down.

_____

_____

7. His father couldn't find another job. The economy was bad.

_____

_____

8. Today, Pete is happy. His father found a new job.

_____

_____

14 **What Do You Think?**

What do you think Pete will do now? Why?

13g Adverb Clauses with *Although* and *Even Though*

Form

Although he has a car, he uses inline skates in the city.

1. *Although* and *even though* are conjunctions that can begin an adverb clause.

2. Like clauses with *because,* clauses with *although* and *even though* can come at the beginning or at the end of a sentence. If they come at the beginning of a sentence, we put a comma after the clause.

He went to work **although he was sick.**
Although he was sick, he went to work.

1. *Although* and *even though* have the same meaning.

   Although he was sick, he went to work.
   Even though he was sick, he went to work.

2. We use *although* and *even though* to show contrast or an unexpected result.

   Even though it was snowing, the road was clear.
   Although it was cold, he wasn't wearing a coat.

15 Practice

Complete the sentences using *who* for people, *that* for things, *because,* and *although*. Add commas where necessary.

J. Paul Getty became a millionaire when he was 24. _____*Although*_____ his father

                                                           1

was rich he did not help his son. Getty was a hard worker _____ made his

       2

money from oil. _____ Getty was a millionaire he wasn't happy.

     3

_____ he married five times he was not happy. _____ he

   4   5

had five children, he didn't love them.

For a man _____ was the richest man in the world at one time, he was

            6

tight with his money. _____ he was an American he loved to live in

       7

England. He bought a house in England _____ had 72 bedrooms, but it had

               8

pay phones in the bedrooms _____ Getty wanted to save money on phone

         9

bills. _____ he was very rich he wrote down every dollar he spent every

   10

evening. _____ he could eat anything he wanted he ate simple food.

    11

_____ Getty didn't like to spend money he bought beautiful and

   12

expensive pieces of art. _____ he loved art he didn't care about the price.

      13

Today, the wonderful pieces of art _____ he bought are in a museum. It is

      14

a museum _____ is in California. It is one of the most famous museums in

    15

the United States. It is called the J. Paul Getty Museum.

Describe a photo of your family or friends.

Step 1. Bring a photo of some of your family and/or friends to class. Tell your partner about the photo.

1. Who is in the photo?
2. Where was the photo taken?
3. How are the people related to you/how do you know the people?
4. What are their physical characteristics?
5. What are their personalities like?
6. What are they studying, or what do they do for a living?

Step 2. Write a sentence or two about the place in the photo.

Examples:

The photo shows the house that I grew up in. Although it is small, we all like it.

Step 3. Write a sentence or two about each person in the photo. Use *who, whom, whose, that, which, because, even though,* or *although*.

Examples:

There is a cake because it is my birthday. The person who is next to me is my aunt. That's the aunt whose husband is a doctor.

Step 4. Write a paragraph about the photo. Write a title in three or four words. For more writing guidelines, see pages 216–220.

Step 5. Evaluate your paragraph.

Checklist

_____ Did you give your paragraph a title?

_____ Did you indent your paragraph?

_____ Did you describe the people and the place in the photo?

Step 6. Work with a partner or your teacher to correct grammar, spelling, and punctuation.

Step 7. Write your final copy.

A   Choose the best answer, A, B, C, or D, to complete the sentence. Mark your answer by darkening the oval with the same letter.

1. Beethoven was a great composer _____ deaf for much of his life.

   A. who was   Ⓐ Ⓑ Ⓒ Ⓓ
   B. whose
   C. who's
   D. whom was

2. The largest animal _____ on land is the elephant.

   A. that live   Ⓐ Ⓑ Ⓒ Ⓓ
   B. that lives
   C. who lives
   D. whom live

3. Louis Pasteur was a French professor _____ showed that germs cause many diseases.

   A. whom   Ⓐ Ⓑ Ⓒ Ⓓ
   B. who was
   C. whose
   D. who

4. The panda is an animal _____ only food is the bamboo plant.

   A. that   Ⓐ Ⓑ Ⓒ Ⓓ
   B. which is
   C. whose
   D. which

5. People _____ money to charity are called donors.

   A. whom give   Ⓐ Ⓑ Ⓒ Ⓓ
   B. who gives
   C. which give
   D. who give

6. A barometer is an instrument _____ air pressure.

   A. who measures   Ⓐ Ⓑ Ⓒ Ⓓ
   B. that measures
   C. which measure
   D. whose measures

7. The blue whale is the largest animal _____.

   A. who lives   Ⓐ Ⓑ Ⓒ Ⓓ
   B. that live
   C. that lives
   D. whom lives

8. Biographies are books _____ the stories of people's lives.

   A. that tell   Ⓐ Ⓑ Ⓒ Ⓓ
   B. whom tell
   C. that tells
   D. who tells

9. Thomas A. Watson was the first person _____ Alexander Graham Bell talked on the first telephone call.

   A. whom   Ⓐ Ⓑ Ⓒ Ⓓ
   B. who to
   C. to whom
   D. whom to

10. We have seasons _____ the Earth goes around the sun.

   A. although   Ⓐ Ⓑ Ⓒ Ⓓ
   B. because
   C. who
   D. that

B Find the underlined word A, B, C, or D, that is incorrect. Mark your answer by darkening the oval with the same letter.

1. There are many flowers who close up
   A   B   C
   at night.
   D

   Ⓐ Ⓑ Ⓒ Ⓓ

2. Because he was famous and talented,
   A   B
   Mozart died poor and alone.
          C   D

   Ⓐ Ⓑ Ⓒ Ⓓ

3. When people get older, their lungs get
                          A
   darker although they breathe dirty air.
          B   C   D

   Ⓐ Ⓑ Ⓒ Ⓓ

4. Picasso was a Spanish artist whom is the
                 A   B   C
   best known 20th Century painter.
                    D

   Ⓐ Ⓑ Ⓒ Ⓓ

5. Egypt is a country in Africa who's capital
   A   B   C
   is Cairo.
   D

   Ⓐ Ⓑ Ⓒ Ⓓ

6. Mark Twain was an American writer whom
                    A   B
   real name was Samuel Clemens.
   C   D

   Ⓐ Ⓑ Ⓒ Ⓓ

7. African elephants have large ears who
                      A   B
   help them to keep cool in the hot climate.
   C   D

   Ⓐ Ⓑ Ⓒ Ⓓ

8. The holiday who is on the fourth Thursday
                A   B
   in November is Thanksgiving Day.
   C   D

   Ⓐ Ⓑ Ⓒ Ⓓ

9. Because so much of the Amazon forest
   A
   has been destroyed, it is still the biggest
                       B   C
   forest in the world.
          D

   Ⓐ Ⓑ Ⓒ Ⓓ

10. Palm trees are not like other trees
               A   B
    although they do not grow side branches.
    C   D

    Ⓐ Ⓑ Ⓒ Ⓓ

UNIT 14

REPORTED SPEECH AND CONDITIONAL CLAUSES

14a Quoted Speech

Elvis said, "I don't know anything about music. In my line, you don't have to."

Quoted speech tells who said something and what they said.

1. We can put the name of the speaker at the beginning of the sentence.

    ```
        A    C                              F
        |    |                              |
    Elvis said, "In my line, you don't have to."
             |         |                    |
             B         D                    E
    ```

    A. Mention the speaker and use a verb like *said*.
    B. Put a comma after the verb.
    C. Open the quotation marks (").
    D. Write the quotation. Capitalize the first word.
    E. End the quotation with a period, a question mark, or an exclamation point.
    F. Close the quotation marks (").

2. We can also put the name of the speaker at the end of the sentence.

    ```
    A                        C    E
    |                        |    |
    "In my line, you don't have to," Elvis said.
                  |              |       |
                  B              D       F
    ```

    A. Open the quotation marks.
    B. Write the quotation. Capitalize the first word.
    C. If the original quotation ended in a period, use a comma at the end. If it ended in a question mark or an exclamation point, use those punctuation marks.
    D. Close the quotation marks.
    E. Mention the speaker and use a word like *said*.
    F. End the sentence with a period.

3. We can also put the name of the speaker after *said*.

   "In my line, you don't have to," said Elvis.

4. If there is more than one sentence in the quotation, we put quotation marks only at the beginning and at the end of the whole quotation. We do not use separate quotation marks for each sentence.

   CORRECT: My mother said, "Elvis was my favorite singer when I was young. He changed my world."
   INCORRECT: My mother said, "Elvis was my favorite singer when I was young." "He changed my world."

Function

We use quoted speech for the exact words someone uses. We use quoted speech in novels, stories, and newspaper articles.

Source	Example
A newspaper article	"I'm retiring at the end of the season," the star player said.
A story about Thomas Edison	Edison said, "I have not failed. I've just found 10,000 ways that won't work."

1 Practice

Nasreddin Hoca (Hodja) is a character in Turkish folktales. Write quoted speech for the speaker's words in this story. Use the verb *said* and the correct punctuation.

Nasreddin had a leaky ferry boat and used it to row people across the river. One day his passenger was a fussy schoolteacher, and on the way across the teacher decided to give Nasreddin a test to see how much he knew.

1. The schoolteacher: Tell me, Nasreddin, what are eight times six?

   The schoolteacher said, "Tell me, Nasreddin, what are eight times six?"

2. Nasreddin: I have no idea.

   _____

3. The schoolteacher: How do you spell *magnificence?*

   _____

4. Nasreddin: I don't know.

   _____

5. The schoolteacher: Didn't you study anything at school?

_____

6. Nasreddin: No.

_____

7. The schoolteacher: In that case, half your life is lost.

_____

Just then, there was a very bad storm, and the boat began to go down.

8. Nasreddin: Tell me, schoolteacher, did you ever learn to swim?

_____

9. The schoolteacher: No.

_____

10. Nasreddin: In that case, your whole life is lost.

_____

14b Reported Speech

Muhammed Ali said that he was the greatest.

1. Reported speech has a main clause and a noun clause.

2. We use reporting verbs such as _say_ or _tell_ in the main clause.

MAIN CLAUSE		NOUN CLAUSE	
Speaker	Reporting Verb	(That)	Reported Speech
Muhammad Ali	said	(that)	he was the greatest.
Mary	says	(that)	she is happy.

3. We can leave out *that*.

> Muhammed Ali said **that** he was the greatest.
> OR Muhammed Ali said he was the greatest.

4. If the reporting verb is in the present tense, there is no change in tense of the verb in the noun clause.

> QUOTED SPEECH: Mary says, "I **am** happy."
> REPORTED SPEECH: Mary **says** that she **is** happy.

5. If the reporting verb is in the past (for example, *said, told*) the verb tense in the noun clause changes when we report it. Some modal auxiliaries change, too.

> QUOTED SPEECH: Muhammad Ali said, "I **am** the greatest."
> REPORTED SPEECH: Muhammad Ali **said** that he **was** the greatest.

This chart shows the tense changes.

QUOTED SPEECH		REPORTED SPEECH	
Verb Tense or Modal	Example	Verb	Example
Simple Present	He said, "I **do** the work."	Simple Past	He said that he **did** the work.
Present Progressive	He said, "I **am doing** the work."	Past Progressive	He said that he **was doing** the work.
Simple Past	He said, "I **did** the work."	Past Perfect	He said that he **had done** the work.
Past Progressive	He said, "I **was doing** the work."	Past Perfect Progressive	He said that he **had been doing** the work.
Present Perfect	He said, "I **have done** the work."	Past Perfect	He said that he **had done** the work.
Future with *Be Going To*	He said, "I **am going** to do the work."	Simple Past for *Be* (*Going To*)	He said that he **was going to do** the work.
Future with *Will*	He said, "I **will do** the work."	Would	He said that he **would do** the work.
Can	He said, "I **can do** the work."	Could	He said that he **could do** the work.
Have to	He said, "I **have to do** the work."	Had to	He said that he **had to do** the work.
Must	He said, "I **must do** the work."	Had to	He said that he **had to do** the work.

Reported Speech and Conditional Clauses

6. There are many possible pronoun changes in reported speech. We use the logic of each situation to decide on the changes.

QUOTED SPEECH: Bob said to Alice, "**You** gave me the wrong book."
REPORTED SPEECH: Bob said that **she** had given him the wrong book.

QUOTED SPEECH: Bob said to me, "**You** gave me the wrong book."
REPORTED SPEECH: Bob said that **I** had given him the wrong book.

The following are some pronoun changes.

PRONOUN CHANGES		
Subject Pronouns	I, you (singular)	he, she, I
	we, you (plural)	they, we
Object Pronouns	me, you (singular)	him, her, me
	you (plural)	us, them
	us (plural)	them

7. Time expressions can change in reported speech.

QUOTED SPEECH: Jim said, "**Tomorrow** is my birthday."
REPORTED SPEECH: Jim said that his birthday was **the next day.**

TIME EXPRESSION CHANGES	
Quoted Speech	Reported Speech
now	then, at that time
today, tonight	that day, that night
yesterday	the day before
tomorrow	the next day
this week	that week
last week	the week before
next week	the week after
two weeks ago	two weeks before

Function

We use reported speech when we report what someone says or said. We use it when we do not want to use the exact words. We use reported speech often in both speech and writing.

2 Practice

Rewrite the sentences as reported speech. Make the necessary changes to verbs and pronouns. In some cases, there is no tense change.

1. Ben says, "I love swimming."

   Ben says that he loves swimming.

2. Kate says, "I can't swim, but I can ride a bicycle."

   _____

3. The newspaper article says, "Swimming is an excellent sport."

   _____

4. Dr. Carter said, "You have to do some exercise every day."

   _____

5. He said, "Twenty minutes a day is enough."

   _____

6. My mother said, "I can walk a lot."

   _____

7. My father said, "I'll go to the gym tomorrow."

   _____

8. Alice said, "I can go with you."

   _____

9. Tony said, "I went to the gym yesterday."

   _____

10. Paul said, "I have been to the gym this week."

    _____

11. Suzy said, "I go every day."

    _____

3 Your Turn

Make up two events that could happen in a country's government. They don't have to be true. They can be funny. Write them on a piece of paper and give it to the teacher. The teacher will distribute the pieces of paper to the class. Using reported speech, tell the class what the headlines say.

Example:
The president's dog bit a reporter.
You: It says that the president's dog bit a reporter.

14c *Say* or *Tell*

A: **Tell me,** Sandy, what did he **say** on the show?
B: He didn't **say anything.** He **said good evening.**
Then he **said a few words** about how happy he
was to be the host of the show. Then he **told
us** a funny story about his girlfriend.
A: That's me, Sandy. That's me!

1. We use *say* with or without a prepositional phrase with *to*.
   CORRECT: Linda said that she was thirsty.
   CORRECT: Linda said **to me** that she was thirsty.
   INCORRECT: Linda ~~said me~~ that she was thirsty.

2. We always use *tell* with an object. We do not use a propositional phrase with *to*
   after *tell*.
   CORRECT: Linda told **me** that she was thirsty.
   INCORRECT: Linda ~~told that~~ she was thirsty.
   INCORRECT: Linda ~~told to me~~ that she was thirsty.

3. We use *say* and *tell* with some special expressions.

Say	Tell
Say something/anything/nothing	Tell the truth/a lie
Say one's prayers	Tell a story/a secret
Say a few words	Tell the time
Say good morning/good afternoon/etc.	Tell the difference

4 | Practice

Complete the sentences with *say* or *tell* in the correct tense.

A.

"No talking Jimmy," the teacher _____said_____ . "I didn't _____ anything,"
                                             1   2

Jimmy _____ the teacher. "Don't _____ lies," the teacher _____ .
               3   4   5

"I can _____ the difference when someone talks and when someone doesn't talk,"
               6

the teacher _____ the class. "Now, I don't want to hear a sound. Is that clear?"
                       7

the teacher _____ .
                   8

B.

"Yesterday Meg _____ she was moving to Alaska," Karen _____ . "She
                       1   2

_____ me that she had found a good job there."
      3

"I don't believe that," Mike _____ . "Last month she _____ me she
                                4   5

was going to Paris. She doesn't _____ the truth all the time, you know."
                                6

C.

Today, my neighbor _____ good morning to me as usual. Then she
                           1

_____ me a story about a mouse in her bedroom last night. She _____
     2   3

that the mouse had run out of her apartment and into my apartment. Did she

_____ me the truth or did she _____ me a story as usual?
     4   5

5 | Your Turn

Work with a partner. Tell your partner a short sentence. It does not have to be true. Your partner tells the class what you told him or her.

Example:
You: I have six children.
Your partner: My partner told me she had six children.

14d Reported Questions

The president of the company **wanted to know why** everybody was sitting so far away from him.

1. Reported questions have a main clause and a noun clause.

MAIN CLAUSE		NOUN CLAUSE		
Subject	Reporting Verb	Wh- Word	Subject	Verb
He	asked	why	everyone	had left.

2. We use verbs like *ask, inquire,* and *wonder* or the expression *want to know* to report questions. We do not use *say* or *tell*.

> "Where do you live?" she **asked** me.
> She **asked** me where I lived.
> She **wanted to know** where I lived.
> She **wondered** where I lived.

3. When the question begins with a wh- word like *who, what, where, when,* and *how,* the noun clause in the reported question begins with the same word.

> He asked me, "**What** do you want?"
> He asked me **what** I wanted.

4. When the question is a yes/no question, we begin the noun clause in the reported question with *if* or *whether*. *If* and *whether* have the same meaning here.

> "Are you coming?" he asked.
> He asked **if** I was coming. OR He asked **whether** I was coming.

5. In reported questions, the words are in statement form. They are not in question form. We do not use question marks.

> He asked me, "How are you?"
> He asked me how I was.
>
> "Are you happy?" she asked us.
> She asked us if we were happy.
>
> "Where is your backpack?" she asked.
> She asked where my backpack was.

6. Reported questions use the same rules as reported speech for changing verb tenses, modal auxiliaries, and other words. Review these rules on pages 177–178.

6 Practice

I was a tourist in London last summer. I met a woman who asked me some questions. Write her questions as reported questions.

1. Can you speak English?

   She asked me if I could speak English.

2. Where do you come from?

   _____

3. Where do you want to go?

   _____

4. Do you have a map?

   _____

5. Have you seen Buckingham Palace?

   _____

6. Did you visit the British Museum?

   _____

7. Is this your first time in London?

   _____

8. What is your name?

   _____

9. Are you married?

   _____

10. Are you on vacation here?

   _____

11. How long are you going to stay here?

_____

12. Would you like to have a cup of tea with me?

_____

7 Practice

Yesterday you saw a man who was lying on the sidewalk. You went to help him and asked some questions. You are reporting what you asked.

1. Are you OK?

I asked if he was OK.

2. Do you need help?

_____

3. How did you fall?

_____

4. Can you stand up?

_____

5. Were you on your way to work?

_____

6. Where does it hurt?

_____

7. What's your name?

_____

8. Can I call someone for you?

_____

9. Do you want me to call for an ambulance?

_____

8 Your Turn

Write five questions to ask your partner. Your partner will answer your questions. Later, your partner will report to the class what you wanted to know and the answer.

Example:

You: Where do you live?
Your partner: I live on Elm Street.
Your partner: My partner wanted to know where I lived. I said that I lived on Elm Street.

14e Reported Commands, Requests, Advice, and Suggestions

The man said, "Stop."
The man **ordered me to stop.**

To report commands, requests, and advice, we can use reporting verb + someone + (*not*) infinitive.

1. We can report commands with the reporting verbs *tell* or *order* + someone + (*not*) infinitive.

    "Don't talk!" the teacher said to us.
    The teacher **told us not to talk.**
    OR The teacher **ordered us not to talk.**

    "Stay in the car," the police officer said.
    The police officer **ordered me to stay** in the car.
    OR The police officer **told me to stay** in the car.

    We can also use the reporting verb *warn* to report commands. We use *warn* to show that something is dangerous.

    "Don't go near the swimming pool!" she said to the little girl.
    She **warned the little girl not to go** near the swimming pool.

2. We can report requests with the reporting verb *ask*.

    "Wait a minute, please," Ted said.
    Ted **asked me to wait** a minute.

    "Would you help me?" he asked.
    He **asked me to help** him.

3. We can report advice with the reporting verb *advise*.

> The doctor said, "Helen, you should lose ten pounds."
> The doctor **advised Helen to lose** ten pounds.

4. There are other verbs that can use the verb + someone + (*not*) infinitive pattern. Here are some of them.

Verb	Example
beg	"Please help me," he said. He **begged me to** help him.
invite	"Will you come to the party?" she said. She **invited me to** come to the party.
offer	"Shall I carry your suitcase?" he said. He **offered to** carry my suitcase.
allow	"You can go early," the teacher said. The **teacher allowed us to** go early.

5. We can use two different structures for reporting suggestions.

SUGGEST + VERB -*ING*			
Quoted Speech	Subject	*Suggest*	Verb -*ing*	
"Let's start early," he said.	He	**suggested**	**starting**	early.

SUGGEST + NOUN CLAUSE			
Quoted Speech	Subject	*Suggest*	(*That*)	Subject + a Base Verb
"Let's start early," he said.	He	**suggested**	**(that)**	**we start** early.

When we use *suggest* + a noun clause, we always use a base verb in the main clause, even for the subjects *he, she,* and *it*.

> CORRECT: The doctor suggested that she **get** more exercise.
> INCORRECT: The doctor suggested that she ~~gets~~ more exercise.

The verb *recommend* also uses these structures:

> The doctor **recommended drinking** a lot of water.
> The doctor **recommended that she drink** a lot of water.

Practice

Complete the sentences with one of the verbs in the list. Use the past tense of the verb. In some sentences, there is more than one correct answer.

advise	beg	warn
allow	invite	
ask	order	

1. "Don't sit on that chair!" the teacher said. "It might break," he added.

   The teacher _____*warned*_____ her not to sit on the chair.

2. "Write your essay," the teacher said.

   The teacher _____ us to write the essay.

3. "Please help me with this question," Kate said to her partner in class. "I really need your help."

   She _____ her partner to help her with that question.

4. "Would you like to have a cup of coffee with me after class?" Tony said to Nancy.

   Tony _____ Nancy to have a cup of coffee with him after class.

5. "You can use your dictionaries to write the essay," the teacher said.

   The teacher _____ us to use our dictionaries to write the essay.

6. "You should write a title for the essay," Tony told Kate. "The teacher likes us to write titles."

   Tony _____ Kate to write a title for the essay.

7. "Please, please, check this essay, " Suzy said to Kim.

   Suzy _____ Kim to check her essay.

8. "You should check the spelling of these words," Kim said to Suzy.

   Kim _____ Suzy to check the spelling of those words.

9. "Do you need any help?" the teacher said to Suzy.

   The teacher _____ Suzy if she needed any help.

10. "You can finish the essay at home," the teacher said.

    The teacher _____ us to finish the essay at home.

Practice

Choose a reporting verb and report the speaker's words.

1. "Let's go to the shopping mall," said Dick to Mary.

   Dick suggested that they go to the shopping mall.

2. "Please, please, give me the keys to the car," Mary said to her brother Dick.

Mary _____

3. "OK, you can drive the car," Dick said to his sister.

Dick _____

4. "Don't drive too fast," Dick said.

_____

5. "Please don't tell Dad," Mary said.

Mary _____

6. "You should be very careful!" said Dick.

_____

7. "Take your driver's license with you," said Dick.

_____

8. "You can drive to the shopping mall," said Dick.

_____

9. "Please, please, let me drive back, too," said Mary.

_____

10. "Let's drive to the mall first," said Dick.

_____

II Practice

Paul is going on vacation for two weeks. He wants people to help him take care of things. Choose a reporting verb and report the speaker's words.

1. Paul said to John, "Can you take care of my bird?"

Paul asked John to take care of his bird.

2. Paul said, "Don't give the bird any cookies."

_____

3. Paul said to Linda, "Will you water my plants for me?"

_____

4. Paul said to Linda, "Don't water them too much."

_____

5. Paul said to his mother, "Please do my laundry."

_____

6. Paul said to his mother, "Don't clean my apartment."

_____

7. Paul said to his mother, "Don't touch my CD player."

_____

8. Paul said to Ken, "Will you give these papers to my boss?"

_____

| 12 | **Your Turn** |

What do you ask people to do for you when you go away? Say three things.

Example:
I ask someone to take my mail into the apartment.

14f Wishes about the Present or Future

Form / Function

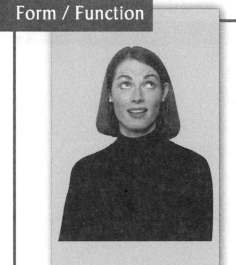

I **wish** I **were** on vacation.

1. We use _wish_ + the simple past to say that we would like something to be different in the present.

> I **wish** I **had** a credit card. (But I don't have a credit card.)
> I **wish** I **made** more money. (But I don't make more money.)

MAIN CLAUSE		NOUN CLAUSE	
Subject	_Wish_	(That)	Subject + Simple Past Verb
I	wish		I **had** a car.
My brother	wishes		he **spoke** Thai.
She	wishes	(that)	she **didn't need** to borrow money.
My parents	wish		they **didn't live** in a small town.
Laura	wishes		she **could go** to Florida for her vacation.*

*We use _could_ after _wish_ to express ability.

189

2. For the verb *to be,* we use *were* for all subjects.*

MAIN CLAUSE		NOUN CLAUSE		
Subject	*Wish*	*(That)*	Subject	*Were/Weren't*
I	wish	that	I	**were** on the beach now.
You			you	**weren't** in class now.
He/She/It	wishes		he/she/it	
We	wish		we	
They			they	

*In informal English, many people use *was* for the subjects *I, he, she,* and *it.*

13 Practice

A. Look at the information in the box. Then write sentences about Carol Brown's wishes.

Reality	Wish
1. has curly hair	have straight hair
2. is short	be tall
3. is a student	be a model
4. makes little money	make a lot of money
5. shares a small apartment	live in a big house
6. rides a bicycle	drive a sports car
7. stays home on weekends	go out with friends on weekends
8. wears regular clothes	wear designer clothes

1. *Carol wishes she had straight hair.*
2. _____
3. _____
4. _____
5. _____
6. _____
7. _____
8. _____

B. Write two more things she wishes.

1. _____
2. _____

14 Practice

Susan started studying at a college far from home. She is not very happy. She wishes things were different. Write sentences about what she wishes.

1. Classes are so hard.

   She wishes classes were not so hard.

2. There are so many tests.

   _____

3. Books are so expensive.

   _____

4. Teachers are not friendly.

   _____

5. I don't have friends.

   _____

6. My roommate is not nice.

   _____

7. I have no time to have fun.

   _____

15 Practice

Nick is a famous soap opera star on television. He doesn't like his present life. He wishes it were different. Write his wishes.

1. Photographers follow me everywhere.

   I wish photographers didn't follow me everywhere.

2. Newspapers write untrue stories about me.

   _____

3. I don't have privacy.

   _____

4. People touch me and pull my clothes.

   _____

5. I have to sign autographs all the time.

   _____

6. I have to smile all the time.

   _____

7. I can't wear anything I want.

   _____

8. I can't go to the store to get groceries.

   _____

16 Your Turn

Do you wish things were different? Give two examples for each wish.

Example:
I wish I had a million dollars.
I wish I had a girlfriend.

1. I wish I had ...
2. I wish I could ...
3. I wish I were ...

14g Wishes about the Past

I **wish** I **had called** yesterday!

We use *wish* + the past perfect tense to make a wish about something in the past that we regret. We cannot change what happened.

I **wish** I **had listened** to you. (I didn't listen to you.)
I **wish** I **had studied** for the test. (I didn't study for the test.)

17 Practice

John went for an interview yesterday. He thinks he didn't get the job. Write sentences about what he wishes about the past.

1. I was so nervous.

   I wish I had not been so nervous.

2. My hands were sweaty.

   _____

3. I didn't look the interviewer in the eye.

   _____

4. I asked about the pay.

   _____

5. I didn't look confident.

   _____

6. I didn't smile.

_____

7. I forgot the name of my last boss.

_____

8. I didn't tell the interviewer about my computer skills.

_____

18 Practice

Alice and Steve met at a party yesterday. Read the sentences about Alice and Steve and write sentences about what they wish they had or had not done.

Steve says to himself:

1. I didn't give her my phone number.

   I wish I had given her my phone number.

2. I didn't ask her what her last name was.

_____

3. I told her that she looked sad.

_____

4. I didn't ask her to dance with me.

_____

Alice says to herself:

5. I didn't tell him my last name.

_____

6. I wasn't very friendly with him.

_____

7. I told him I was tired.

_____

8. I told him I was with a friend.

_____

9. I left early.

_____

10. I didn't give him a chance.

_____

19 **Your Turn**

What did you do or not do last week? Are there things you wish you had done or hadn't done? Say three things.

Example:
I wish I hadn't spent so much money.
I wish I had seen that program on TV.

14h Present Real Conditional and Future Conditional Sentences

Form

If you see a koala bear outside of a zoo, you are in Australia.

1. We use two clauses in a conditional sentence, an *if* clause and a main clause. The *if* clause contains the condition and the main clause contains the result.

Type of Sentence	Form	*If* Clause	Main Clause
Present Real Conditional	Simple present tense in both clauses	If you **see** a koala bear outside of a zoo,	you **are** in Australia.
		If the temperature **doesn't fall** below 0° C,	water **won't freeze.**
Future Conditional	*If* **clause:** Simple present tense **Main clause:** Future tense	If I **miss** the bus,	I **will be** late.
		If he **doesn't study,**	he **won't get** a good grade.

195

Reported Speech and Conditional Clauses

2. We can put the *if* clause first or the main clause first. There is no difference in meaning. When we put the *if* clause first, we put a comma after it.

> **If I miss the bus,** I will be late.
> OR I will be late **if I miss the bus.**

3. In the main clause of a future conditional sentence, we can use any verb form that refers to the future.

> If I finish my homework soon, I **can go** to bed.
> If my sister visits me, we**'re going to travel** around the country.

Function

1. We use the present real conditional to talk about what happens when there is a definite situation.

> If I have a big lunch, it makes me sleepy.
> If she hears his name, she gets angry.

2. We use the present real conditional to talk about general facts that are always true.

> If an elephant has big ears, it comes from Africa.
> If you mix oil and water, the oil stays on top.

3. We use the present real conditional to talk about habits or things that happen every day.

> If I go to work by car, it takes thirty-five minutes.
> I always walk to the store if it doesn't rain.

4. We use the future conditional to make predictions about what will happen in the future.

> If it rains tomorrow, we'll visit a museum.
> If he comes early, we'll go out.

20 Practice

Complete the sentences with the correct tense of the verb in parentheses.

1. If people sneeze, they (close) _____*close*_____ their eyes.

2. If you (exercise) _____ a lot, you lose weight.

3. You die if you (not/get) _____ oxygen.

4. If you (break) _____ a nail, it grows back again.

5. People (sweat) _____ if they exercise.

6. If you (cut) _____ your finger, it bleeds.

21 Practice

What will you see if you and your family go to these places? Write sentences with the prompts. Use the correct punctuation.

1. London/Buckingham Palace

   If we go to London, we will see Buckingham Palace.

2. Paris/the Eiffel Tower

   _____

3. Rome/the Coliseum

   _____

4. New York/the Statue of Liberty

   _____

5. Egypt/the pyramids

   _____

6. Los Angeles/the movie studios

   _____

7. Sydney/the Sydney Opera House

   _____

8. Venice/gondolas

   _____

9. Tokyo/the Imperial Gardens

   _____

10. Mexico City/the Archaeological Museum

   _____

22 Practice

What will happen if...? Sandra's mother always worries about her when she is away from home. Match the sentence parts. Then write the sentences below. Use the correct punctuation.

__c__	**1.** eat too much	**a.**	feel better
_____	**2.** lie in the sun	**b.**	catch a cold
_____	**3.** drink too much coffee	**c.**	gain weight
_____	**4.** don't eat breakfast	**d.**	not be tired in the morning
_____	**5.** go without a coat	**e.**	get sunburned
_____	**6.** go to sleep early	**f.**	not sleep
_____	**7.** take this medicine	**g.**	be hungry

1. _If she eats too much, she will gain weight._ _____

2. _____

3. _____

4. _____

5. _____

6. _____

7. _____

23 Practice

Use the verb form for the present real conditional (simple present) if it is possible in the sentence. If it is not possible, use the verb form for the future conditional (future tense).

René's parents are coming to visit him in the United States.

1. My parents are coming for a visit next week. If we have enough time, we (visit)

_____ _will visit_ _____ the art museum.

2. If they don't like the art museum, we (go) _____ shopping at a mall.

3. We can't stay at the mall for a long time because my mother has problems with her feet. If she walks too much, her feet (hurt) _____.

4. If it doesn't rain, we (rent) _____ a boat and row on the lake.

5. My father likes boats. If he is on a boat, he (be) _____ happy.

6. As for me, if I don't take a pill, I (get) _____ sick when I'm on a boat.

7. There is a concert at the university. If I can get tickets, we (go)

   _____.

8. My parents like trying new food. If they have a choice, they (eat)

   _____ food from different countries.

9. If we go to Chinatown, they (love) _____ the food there.

10. If they have a good time this year, they (come) _____ back

    next year.

11. If I get to see my parents once a year, I (be) _____ lucky.

24 Your Turn

Answer what you will do if the following things happen.

Example:
if you pass this class with an A
If I pass this class with an A, I'll have a big party.

1. if you pass this class with an A
2. if it rains tomorrow
3. if there is no class tomorrow

14i Present Unreal Conditional Sentences

Form

If **I had** a million dollars,
I **would buy** an island in
the sun.

IF CLAUSE			MAIN CLAUSE		
If	Subject	Past Tense Verb	Subject	*Would/ Could*	Base Verb
If	I	**had** a lot of money, **were** very rich,	I	**would**	**buy** that big house.
	you		you	**'d**	
	he		he	**wouldn't**	
	she		she		
	we		we	**could**	
	they		they	**couldn't**	

Remember, after *if*, we use *were* for all persons.

If she **were** a millionaire, would she be happy?

Function

We use *if* + simple past + *would/could* + base verb for an unreal situation in the present. The statement is contrary to fact. We imagine a result in the present or future.

If I **had** a million dollars, **I'd be** very happy. (I don't have a million dollars.)
If you **wrote** things down, you **wouldn't forget** them. (You don't write things down, and you always forget them.)

25 Practice

Complete the sentences with the correct form of the present unreal conditional verb in parentheses.

A.

If my car (break) _____*broke*_____ down on the highway at night, I
                         1

(lock) _____ the doors. Then, I (call) _____ for emergency
         2   **3**

services on my cell phone. If I (not have) _____ a cell phone, I
                                              4

(walk) _____ to the nearest emergency call box. If the emergency call box
         5

(be) _____ too far away, I (wait) _____ in my car with my
       6   **7**

doors locked.

B.

If someone (steal) _____ my purse with all my money and credit cards
                      1

in it, I (report) _____ it to the police. Then, I (call) _____
                    2   **3**

the credit card company. If I (think) _____ I could find it,
4

I (go) _____ back to all the places to look for it.
5

C.

If I (see) _____ a big spider in my bed, I
1

(scream) _____. If I (be) _____ alone, I
2   3

(find) _____ a friend or neighbor to do something about it. If I
4

(not/find) _____ anyone, I (sleep) _____ in another
5   6

room or maybe not sleep at all!

D.

If I (wake) _____ up in the night and (hear) _____
1   2

something in my house, I (go) _____ to the phone and call the police. If I
3

(be) _____ alone, I (lock) _____ the door of the room, and
4   5

wait for the police to come.

26 Practice

What would you do if these things happened to you? Write your own sentences.

1. If someone called you in the middle of the night

   If someone called me in the middle of the night, I'd get out

   of bed and answer the phone.

2. If all the lights suddenly went out

   _____

   _____

3. If you found a snake in your closet

   _____

   _____

4. If you saw a strange person breaking into your neighbor's house

   _____

   _____

5. If you smelled smoke in your house

   _____

   _____

Ask and answer the questions with a partner.

Example:
You: If you could be someone else, who would you like to be? Why?
Your partner: I'd be Bill Gates because I love computers, and I want to be rich.

1. If you could be someone else, who would you like to be? Why?
2. If you could live somewhere else, where would you like to live? Why?
3. If you could interview someone, who would you like to interview? What questions would you like to ask?

14j Past Unreal Conditional Sentences

Form

If we **had lived** one hundred years ago, we **would have dressed** differently.

	IF CLAUSE		MAIN CLAUSE	
If	Subject	Past Perfect Tense	Subject	*Would/Could/Might +* Have + Past Participle
If	I	**had lived** 100 years ago,	I	**would have worn** different clothes.
	he	**hadn't driven** so fast,	he	**would have passed** the driving test.
	she	**had been** here,	she	**might have gotten** the job.

1. We use the past unreal conditional to talk about what might have been the result if things had been different in the past.

> If I **had studied** harder, I **would have passed** the test.
> (I didn't study harder, and I didn't pass the test.)

> If it **hadn't snowed,** we **might not have had** the accident.
> (It snowed, and we had the accident.)

> If they **had sent** the letter, it **would have arrived** last week.
> (They didn't send the letter, and it didn't arrive last week.)

2. We can use *would, might,* and *could* in the main clause.

We use *would have* + past participle in the main clause if we think the past action was certain.

> If I had heard the telephone ring, I **would have answered** it.
> (I think I would definitely have answered it.)

We use *might have* + past participle in the main clause if we think the past action was possible.

> If you had paid more attention, you **might not have burned** the food.
> (I think it's possible that you wouldn't have burned it.)

We use *could have* + past participle to say that someone would have been able to do something in the past.

> If you had brought your CDs, we **could have danced.**
> (We would have been able to dance.)

---

28 Practice

Complete the sentences with the correct tense of the verb in parentheses.

1. If I (not/get up) _____ *hadn't gotten up* _____ late, I
   (not/miss) _____ *wouldn't have missed* _____ the train.

2. If I (not/miss) _____ the train, I
   (not/be) _____ late for work.

3. If I (not/be) _____ late for work, my boss
   (not/get) _____ angry with me.

4. If my boss (not/get) _____ angry with me, he

(not/yell) _____ at me.

5. If he (not/yell) _____ at me, I

(not/yell) _____ at him.

6. If I (not/yell) _____ at him, I

(not/lose) _____ my job.

29 Practice

Harold is thinking about his past. There are things in his life he wanted to do but did not do.

A. Write sentences to express what he would, might, or could have done if things had been different. You can use *would, might,* or *could.*

1. I wanted to go to the university, but my parents didn't have the money.

If his parents had had the money, he could have gone to the university.

2. I wanted to buy a farm, but I didn't have the money.

_____

_____

3. I asked Nina to marry me, but she didn't like my nose.

_____

_____

4. I wanted to be an actor, but I didn't have enough talent.

_____

_____

5. I wanted to go to Brazil, but I couldn't speak Portuguese.

_____

_____

6. I wanted to work for my uncle, but he died.

_____

_____

7. My uncle was a thoughtful man, so he left a will.

If my uncle hadn't been a thoughtful man, he _____

_____

8. My uncle left a will, and I became a millionaire.

_____

_____

9. I became a millionaire, and Nina married me.

_____

_____

B. Write five sentences about yourself if you had lived 100 years ago. Write about what you would, might, or could (not) have done or had.

1. *If I had lived one hundred years ago, I wouldn't have had a*
  telephone.

2. _____

3. _____

4. _____

5. _____

30 Your Turn

Think about your past. Do you wish that any things had been different? Write five sentences with *wish,* and then write a sentence using the unreal past conditional.

Example:
I wish I had learned to play the guitar. If I had learned how to play the guitar, I could have joined a band.

1. _____

_____

2. _____

_____

3. _____

_____

4. _____

_____

5. _____

_____

WRITING: Write a Personal Narrative

Write a diary entry about your mistakes.

Step 1. Imagine that you didn't pass your classes. Think about these questions.
1. Would you have passed if you had studied harder?
2. Why didn't you study harder? What do you regret?
3. What would happen if your parents knew? What would you say to them?
4. What do you wish you could do?

Step 2. Write your answers to these or other questions.

Step 3. Look at the following diary entry. Use your answers in Step 2 to write your diary entry. Use some past unreal conditional sentences in your diary entry. For more writing guidelines, see pages 216–220.

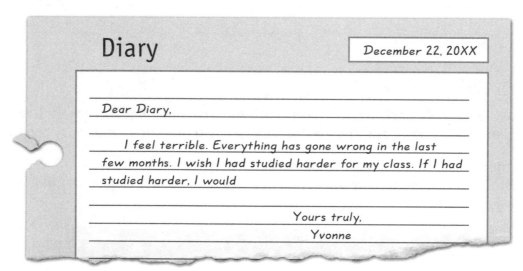

Step 4. Evaluate your diary entry.

Checklist

_____ Did you write a date for your diary entry?

_____ Did you start entry with "Dear Diary" followed by a comma?

_____ Did you indent your paragraphs?

_____ Did you use some past unreal conditional sentences?

_____ Did you end your entry with a closing such as "Yours truly" and a comma?

_____ Did you sign your name at the end?

Step 5. Work with a partner to edit your diary entry. Check spelling, punctuation, vocabulary, and grammar.

Step 6. Write your final diary entry.

A **Choose the best answer, A, B, C, or D, to complete the sentence. Mark your answer by darkening the oval with the same letter.**

1. I wish the sun _____.

   A. is shining   Ⓐ Ⓑ Ⓒ Ⓓ
   B. was shining
   C. were to shine
   D. were shining

2. Kim _____ a funny story last night.

   A. said me   Ⓐ Ⓑ Ⓒ Ⓓ
   B. to me said
   C. told me
   D. tell me

3. Ben said that he _____ with us next week.

   A. will go   Ⓐ Ⓑ Ⓒ Ⓓ
   B. would go
   C. is go
   D. will to go

4. He asked _____.

   A. whether I am coming   Ⓐ Ⓑ Ⓒ Ⓓ
   B. if I am coming
   C. whether I was coming
   D. if I come

5. If I could afford the plane ticket, I _____ on the next plane to Hawaii.

   A. would be   Ⓐ Ⓑ Ⓒ Ⓓ
   B. could have been
   C. will be
   D. were

6. If my father _____ the opportunity, he would have gone to the university.

   A. have   Ⓐ Ⓑ Ⓒ Ⓓ
   B. had
   C. had had
   D. have had

7. She _____ happy, but I wasn't.

   A. asked to me if I was   Ⓐ Ⓑ Ⓒ Ⓓ
   B. asked me if I were
   C. said to me if I was
   D. told me if I was

8. He suggested _____.

   A. going early   Ⓐ Ⓑ Ⓒ Ⓓ
   B. to going early
   C. to go early
   D. us going early

9. I didn't give him my card. I wish I _____ him my card.

   A. give   Ⓐ Ⓑ Ⓒ Ⓓ
   B. have give
   C. had given
   D. had given to

10. If you don't have air to breathe, you _____.

    A. would die   Ⓐ Ⓑ Ⓒ Ⓓ
    B. die
    C. would have died
    D. died

B Find the underlined word or phrase, A, B, C or D, that is incorrect. Mark your answer by darkening the oval with the same letter.

1. If I had <u>a</u> car, I <u>will</u> not <u>use</u> public
   A   B   C   D
   transportation.

   Ⓐ Ⓑ Ⓒ Ⓓ

2. The teacher <u>warned</u> <u>to</u> <u>us</u> not <u>to talk</u>
                 A   B   C   D
   during the test.

   Ⓐ Ⓑ Ⓒ Ⓓ

3. If we had <u>lived</u> a hundred years <u>ago</u>, we
              A   B
   wouldn't <u>had</u> problems with air <u>pollution</u>.
            C   D

   Ⓐ Ⓑ Ⓒ Ⓓ

4. When I was a child, my father <u>told</u> <u>me</u> to
                                  A   B
   <u>always</u> <u>say</u> the truth.
     C   D

   Ⓐ Ⓑ Ⓒ Ⓓ

5. The doctor recommended <u>to</u> using <u>less</u>
                          A   B
   salt and <u>sugar</u> and <u>drinking</u> more water.
            C   D

   Ⓐ Ⓑ Ⓒ Ⓓ

6. I <u>will have</u> health problems <u>if</u> I <u>won't</u>
        A   B   C
   follow <u>this diet</u>.
          D

   Ⓐ Ⓑ Ⓒ Ⓓ

7. My manager <u>said</u> me <u>that</u> he <u>was going</u> on
               A   B   C
   <u>vacation</u> next week.
    D

   Ⓐ Ⓑ Ⓒ Ⓓ

8. The school counselor <u>advised</u> <u>me</u> <u>taking</u>
                         A   B   C
   <u>an</u> English writing class next semester.
    D

   Ⓐ Ⓑ Ⓒ Ⓓ

9. I didn't study English when I <u>was</u> in high
                                 A
   school, but now I <u>wish</u> I <u>have</u> studied <u>it</u>.
                      B   C   D

   Ⓐ Ⓑ Ⓒ Ⓓ

10. <u>If</u> I knew how <u>to speak</u> French, I <u>will</u> go
     A   B   C
    <u>to France</u> with you.
     D

    Ⓐ Ⓑ Ⓒ Ⓓ

APPENDICES

Appendix 1   Grammar Terms

Adjective
An adjective describes a noun or a pronoun.

> My cat is very **intelligent**. He's **orange** and **white**.

Adverb
An adverb describes a verb, another adverb, or an adjective.

> Joey speaks **slowly**. He **always** visits his father on Wednesdays.
>
> His father cooks **extremely** well. His father is a **very** talented chef.

Article
An article comes before a noun. The definite article is *the*. The indefinite articles are *a* and *an*.

> I read **an** online story and **a** magazine feature about celebrity lifestyles.
>
> **The** online story was much more interesting than **the** magazine feature.

Auxiliary Verb
An auxiliary verb is found with a main verb. It is often called a "helping" verb.

> Susan **can't** play in the game this weekend. **Does** Ruth play baseball?

Base Form
The base form of a verb has no tense. It has no endings (*–ed*, *–s*, or *–ing*).

> Jill didn't **see** the band. She should **see** them when they are in town.

Comparative

Comparative forms compare two things. They can compare people, places, or things.

This orange is **sweeter than** that grapefruit.

Working in a large city is **more stressful than** working in a small town.

Conjunction

A conjunction joins two or more sentences, adjectives, nouns, or prepositional phrases. Some conjunctions are *and, but,* and *or.*

Kasey is efficient, **and** her work is excellent.

Her apartment is small **but** comfortable.

She works Wednesdays **and** Thursdays.

Contraction

A contraction is composed of two words put together with an apostrophe. Some letters are left out.

Frank usually **doesn't** answer his phone.	(doesn't = does + not)
He's really busy.	(he's = he + is)
Does he know what time **we're** meeting?	(we're = we + are)

Imperative

An imperative gives a command or directions. It uses the base form of the verb, and it does not use the word *you.*

Go to the corner and **turn** left.

Modal

A modal is a type of auxiliary verb. The modal auxiliaries are *can, could, may, might, must, shall, should, will,* and *would.*

Elizabeth **will** act the lead role in the play next week.

She **couldn't** go to the party last night because she had to practice her lines.

She **may** be able to go to the party this weekend.

Noun

A noun is a person, an animal, a place, or a thing.

My **brother** and **sister-in-law** live in **Pennsylvania**. They have three **cats**.

Object

An object is the noun or pronoun that receives the action of the verb.

Georgie sent **a gift** for Johnny's birthday.

Johnny thanked **her** for the gift.

Preposition

A preposition is a small connecting word that is followed by a noun or pronoun. Some are a*t, above, after, by, before, below, for, in, of, off, on, over, to, under, up,* and *with.*

> Every day, Jay drives Chris and Ally **to** school **in** the new car.
>
> **In** the afternoon, he waits **for** them **at** the bus stop.

Pronoun

A pronoun takes the place of a noun.

> Chris loves animals. **He** has two dogs and two cats.
>
> His pets are very friendly. **They** like to spend time with people.

Sentence

A sentence is a group of words that has a subject and a verb. It is complete by itself.

> Sentence: Brian works as a lawyer.
>
> Not a sentence: Works as a lawyer.

Subject

A subject is the noun or pronoun that does the action in the sentence.

> **Trisha** is from Canada.
>
> **She** writes poetry about nature.

Superlative

Superlative forms compare three or more people, places, or things.

> Jennifer is **the tallest** girl in the class.
>
> She is from Paris, which is **the most romantic** city in the world.

Tense

Tense tells when the action in a sentence happens.

Simple present	–	The cat **eats** fish every morning.
Present progressive	–	He **is eating** fish now.
Simple past	–	He **ate** fish yesterday morning.
Past progressive	–	He **was eating** when the doorbell rang.
Future with *be going to*	–	He **is going to eat** fish tomorrow morning, too!
Future with *will*	–	I think that he **will eat** the same thing next week.

Verb

A verb tells the action in a sentence.

> Melissa **plays** guitar in a band.
>
> She **loves** writing new songs.
>
> The band **has** four other members.

Appendix 2   Irregular Verbs

Base Form	Simple Past	Past Participle	Base Form	Simple Past	Past Participle
be	was, were	been	keep	kept	kept
become	became	become	know	knew	known
begin	began	begun	leave	left	left
bend	bent	bent	lend	lent	lent
bite	bit	bitten	lose	lost	lost
blow	blew	blown	make	made	made
break	broke	broken	meet	met	met
bring	brought	brought	pay	paid	paid
build	built	built	put	put	put
buy	bought	bought	read	read	read
catch	caught	caught	ride	rode	ridden
choose	chose	chosen	ring	rang	rung
come	came	come	run	ran	run
cost	cost	cost	say	said	said
cut	cut	cut	see	saw	seen
do	did	done	sell	sold	sold
draw	drew	drawn	send	sent	sent
drink	drank	drunk	shake	shook	shaken
drive	drove	driven	shut	shut	shut
eat	ate	eaten	sing	sang	sung
fall	fell	fallen	sit	sat	sat
feed	fed	fed	sleep	slept	slept
feel	felt	felt	speak	spoke	spoken
fight	fought	fought	spend	spent	spent
find	found	found	stand	stood	stood
fly	flew	flown	steal	stole	stolen
forget	forgot	forgotten	swim	swam	swum
get	got	gotten/got	take	took	taken
give	gave	given	teach	taught	taught
go	went	gone	tear	tore	torn
grow	grew	grown	tell	told	told
hang	hung	hung	think	thought	thought
have	had	had	throw	threw	thrown
hear	heard	heard	understand	understood	understood
hide	hid	hidden	wake up	woke up	woken up
hit	hit	hit	wear	wore	worn
hold	held	held	win	won	won
hurt	hurt	hurt	write	wrote	written

Appendix 3   Spelling Rules for Endings

Adding a Final –s to Nouns and Verbs

Rule	Example	-s
1. For most words, add –s without making any changes.	book bet save play	books bets saves plays
2. For words ending in a consonant + *y*, change the *y* to *i* and add –es.	study party	studies parties
3. For words ending in *ch*, *s*, *sh*, *x*, or *z*, add –es.	church class wash fix quiz	churches classes washes fixes quizzes
4. For words ending in *o*, sometimes add –es and sometimes add –s.	potato piano	potatoes pianos
5. For words ending in *f* or *lf*, change the *f* or *lf* to *v* and add –es. For words ending in *fe*, change the *f* to *v* and add –s.	loaf half life	loaves halves lives

Adding a Final *-ed*, *-er*, *-est*, and *-ing*

Rule	Example	-ed	-er	-est	-ing
1. For most words, add the ending without making any changes.	clean	cleaned	cleaner	cleanest	cleaning
2. For words ending in silent *e*, drop the *e* and add *-ed*, *-er*, or *-est*.	save like nice	saved liked	saver nicer	 nicest	saving liking
3. For words ending in a consonant + *y*, change the *y* to *i* and add the ending. Do not change or drop the *y* before adding *-ing*.	sunny happy study worry	 studied worried	sunnier happier	sunniest happiest	 studying worrying
4. For one-syllable words ending in one vowel and one consonant, double the final consonant, then add the ending. Do not double the last consonant if it is a *w, x,* or *y.*	hot run bat glow mix stay	 batted glowed mixed stayed	hotter runner batter	hottest	 running batting glowing mixing staying
5. For words of two or more syllables that end in one vowel and one consonant, double the final consonant if the final syllable is stressed.	begin refer occur permit	 referred occurred permitted	beginner		beginning referring occurring permitting
6. For words of two or more syllables that end in one vowel and one consonant, do NOT double the final consonant if the final syllable is NOT stressed.	enter happen develop	entered happened developed	developer		entering happening developing

Appendix 4   Capitalization Rules

First words

1. Capitalize the first word of every sentence.

   They live in San Francisco.   **W**hat is her name?

2. Capitalize the first word of a quotation.

   She said, "**M**y name is Nancy."

Names

1. Capitalize names of people, including titles of address.

   Mr. **T**hompson   **A**lison **E**mmet   **M**ike **A. L**ee

2. Capitalize the word "I".

   Rose and **I** went to the market.

3. Capitalize nationalities, ethnic groups, and religions.

   Latino   **A**sian   **K**orean   **I**slam

4. Capitalize family words if they appear alone or with a name, but not if they have a possessive pronoun or article.

   He's at **A**unt Lucy's house.   vs.   He's at an **a**unt's house.

Places

1. Capitalize the names of countries, states, cities, and geographical areas.

   Tokyo   **M**exico   the **S**outh   **V**irginia

2. Capitalize the names of oceans, lakes, rivers, and mountains.

   the **P**acific **O**cean   **L**ake **O**ntario   **M**t. **E**verest

3. Capitalize the names of streets, schools, parks, and buildings.

   Central **P**ark   **M**ain **S**treet   the **E**mpire **S**tate **B**uilding

4. Don't capitalize directions if they aren't names of geographical areas.

   She lives **n**ortheast of Washington. We fly **s**outh during our flight.

Time words

1. Capitalize the names of days and months.

   Monday   **F**riday   **J**anuary   **S**eptember

2. Capitalize the names of holidays and historical events.

   Christmas   **I**ndependence **D**ay   **W**orld **W**ar I

3. Don't capitalize the names of seasons.

   spring   **s**ummer   **f**all   **w**inter

Titles

1. Capitalize the first word and all important words of titles of books, magazines, newspapers, and articles.

    The Sound and the Fury   *Time Out*   *The New York Times*

2. Capitalize the first word and all important words of titles of films, plays, radio programs, and TV shows.

    Star Wars   "Friends"   *Mid Summer Night's Dream*

3. Don't capitalize articles (*a, an, the*), conjunctions (*but, and, or*) and short prepositions (*of, with, in, on, for*) unless they are the first word of a title.

    The Story of Cats   *The Woman in the Dunes*

Appendix 5   Punctuation Rules

Period

1. Use a period at the end of a statement or command.

    I live in New York.   Open the door.

2. Use a period after most abbreviations.

    Ms.   Dr.   St.   U.S.

    Exceptions: NATO   UN   AIDS   IBM

3. Use a period after initials.

    Ms. K.L. Kim   F.C. Simmons

Question Mark

1. Use a question mark at the end of questions.

    Is he working tonight?   Where did they use to work?

2. In a direct quotation, the question mark goes before the quotation marks.

    Martha asked, "What's the name of the street?"

Exclamation Point

Use an exclamation point at the end of exclamatory sentences or phrases. They express surprise or strong emotion.

    Wow!   I got an A!

Comma

1. Use a comma to separate items in a series.

   John will have juice, coffee, and tea at the party.

2. Use a comma to separate two or more adjectives that each modify the noun alone.

   Purrmaster is a smart, friendly cat. (*smart* and *friendly* cat)

3. Use a comma before a conjunction (*and, but, or, so*) that separates two independent clauses.

   The book is very funny, and the film is funny too.

   She was tired, but she didn't want to go to sleep.

4. Don't use a comma before a conjunction that separates a sentence from an incomplete sentence.

   I worked in a bakery at night and went to class during the day.

5. Use a comma after an introductory clause or phrase.

   After we hike the first part of the trail, we are going to rest.

6. Use a comma after *yes* and *no* in answers.

   Yes, that is my book.

   No, I'm not.

7. Use a comma to separate quotations from the rest of a sentence. Don't use a comma if the quotation is a question and it is in the first part of the sentence.

   The student said, "I'm finished with the homework."

   "Are you really finished?" asked the student.

Apostrophe

1. Use apostrophes in contractions.

   don't (*do not*)   it's (*it is*)   he's (*he is*)   we're (*we are*)

2. Use apostrophes to show possession.

   Anne's book (the book belongs to Anne)

Quotation Marks

1. Use quotation marks at the beginning and end of exact quotations. Other punctuation marks go before the end quotation marks.

   Burt asked, "When are we leaving?"

   "Right after lunch," Mark replied.

2. Use quotation marks before and after titles of articles, songs, stories, and television shows. Periods and commas are usually placed before the end quotation marks, while question marks and exclamation points are placed after them. If the title is a question, the question mark is placed inside the quotation marks, and appropriate punctuation is placed at the end of the sentence.

> Burt's favorite song is "Show Some Emotion" by Joan Armatrading.
> He read an article called "Motivating Your Employees."
> We read an interesting article called "How Do You Motivate Employees?".

Italics and Underlining

1. If you are writing on a computer, use italic type (*like this*) for books, newspapers, magazines, films, plays, and words from other languages.

> Have you ever read *Woman in the Dunes*?
> How do you say *buenos dias* in Chinese?

2. If you are writing by hand, underline the titles of books, newspapers, magazines, films, and plays.

> Have you ever read <u>Woman in the Dunes</u>?
> How do you say <u>buenos dias</u> in Chinese?

Appendix 6   Writing Basics

I. Sentence types

There are three types of sentences: declarative, interrogative, and exclamatory. Declarative sentences state facts and describe events, people, or things. We use a period at the end of these sentences. Interrogative sentences ask yes/no questions and wh- questions. We use a question mark at the end of these sentences. Exclamatory sentences express surprise or extreme emotion, such as joy or fear. We use an exclamation point at the end of these sentences.

2. Indenting

We indent the first line of a paragraph. Each paragraph expresses a new thought, and indenting helps to mark the beginning of this new thought.

3. Writing titles

The title should give the main idea of a piece of writing. It should be interesting. It goes at the top of the composition and is not a complete sentence. In a title, capitalize the first word and all of the important words.

4. Writing topic sentences

The topic sentence tells the reader the main idea of the paragraph. It is always a complete sentence with a subject and a verb. It is often the first sentence in a paragraph, but sometimes it is in another position in the paragraph.

5. Organizing ideas

Information can be organized in a paragraph in different ways. One common way is to begin with a general idea and work toward more specific information. Another way is to give the information in order of time using words like *before, after, as, when, while,* and *then.*

6. Connecting ideas

It is important to connect the ideas in a paragraph so that the paragraph has cohesion. Connectors and transitional words help make the writing clear, natural, and easy to read. Connectors and transitional words include *and, in addition, also, so, but, however, for example, such as, so ... that,* and *besides.*

7. The writing process

Success in writing generally follows these basic steps:

❖ Brainstorm ideas.
❖ Organize the ideas.
❖ Write a first draft of the piece.
❖ Evaluate and edit the piece for content and form.
❖ Rewrite the piece.

Index